Advance Praise for Dyslexia Outside-the-Box

This book really helped sum up all of the basic information I've been trying to gather from various sources. I love how balanced it's presented! It helps me explain what's going on in a way that has made my daughter feel much better about herself! The appendices are incredibly useful. There are so many useful suggestions; I'll definitely be referring back to them over and over again.

~Renee Stollery, parent of a seven-year-old recently diagnosed with dyslexia

Dyslexia Outside-the-Box is chock-full of information and practical ideas I have not read elsewhere – and I have read a lot! While Beth Ellen Nash is an expert in the field of dyslexia, she understands that the parents play an integral role in helping the child succeed. This book arms parents with a plethora of fun and easy suggestions to help a struggling learner.

~Amy Matthys, homeschooling mom of a 13-year-old with dyslexia

Whether newly researching dyslexia, or experienced yourself with the struggles and successes of this often misunderstood "learning differently" disorder, *Dyslexia Outside-the-Box* will give a deeper understanding of dyslexia itself and those who cope and adapt to its challenges. It's time the world learns to appreciate the many talents dyslexics bring to the world; author Beth Ellen Nash helps to open that box!

~Cat Bachhofer, parent of a 12-year-old with dyslexia

This book is a rich, informative, and encouraging look at dyslexia from a new and positive perspective. It is based on years of research and experience, coming from the most passionate teacher we've ever encountered, who refuses to leave any student behind. Wings to Soar Online Academy and this book have been an answer to many prayers for our daughter.

~Katie Keene, homeschooling mom of an 11-year-old with dyslexia

D1451878

Embrace dyslexia! Thank you for the eye opening, and surprisingly positive, look at dyslexia. It brings everything together…individually breaking down the many aspects of dyslexia, while also offering solutions that have the "whole person" in mind. Practical and informative!

~Heather Hoffman, homeschooling parent

This book is fantastic. It's a great resource for everyone and I love the boxes with the bullets. The appendices are like talking to a friend and getting advice. It's well-written and in an understandable way that's not imposing or pushes a view on someone. Every teacher needs to read this! Parents too!

~Dyslexic parent of an 11-year-old with dyslexia

An informative, practical book on dyslexia offering insights and bringing hope to those working with children whose brains are delightfully wired differently.

~Teresa Cicela, homeschooling mom of a 14-year-old dyslexic

The language is not too scientific and that's good for kids whose parents read them the book and also good because it explains the good and bad stuff. It's hard being dyslexic in a world of not dyslexics. Sometimes there are good things about it but things are really hard, like school, and people don't understand.

~Kid author of *Dyslexic Renegade*

Wonderfully and simply written. This book gives parents, educators, and anyone else who knows and wants to support someone with dyslexia information that is written in a way that is truly helpful and informative. Some of the books I have read are entirely too difficult and clinical. This lays it all out, and makes sense.

~Giuliana Domenica, parent of a nine-year-old with dyslexia

I am pleasantly surprised and amazed at the amount of enlightening and helpful information that I found in *Dyslexia Outside-the-Box*. I think this book is a "must have" for anyone who has or loves someone with dyslexia. After sharing it with them, some of my daughters' teachers agree. They can't wait to add it to their "parents' resource center library" (at a school specifically for dyslexia, dysgraphia, etc.).

~Renée Sotelo, Florida, mother of two daughters with dyslexia who also has
five adult dyslexic family members

This book is a must read for all parents who have children with dyslexia. As both a mom and a registered nurse I am very science driven and believe in quality information. This book brings together evidence-based information surrounding dyslexia and puts it together in an organized, easy to understand format. The appendices are filled with important, practical, hands-on details. This book has eased my stress in trying to gain information that I can put to real life use. I needed to understand how my daughter's brain worked so I could align my teaching strategies with her unique strengths.

~Jacqueline Taylor-Freake, RN, and parent of an eight-year-old
(and likely a four-year-old) with dyslexia

A well-researched book on dyslexia with insights into how the minds of those with dyslexia work. There is help and hope for those who struggle with dyslexia!

~Debbie Sasser, homeschooling mom of an eight-year-old

A brilliant insight into dyslexic thinking! As I was reading through the pages, I could recognise the superpowers of my dyslexic daughter. A must-have guide for any non-dyslexic parents who want to understand their child better.

~Jonna Underwood, Australia

A very informative read that helps me understand better the mind of a child with dyslexia. It doesn't talk above me, but explains terms in a way I can easily understand. The appendices are very helpful, including strategies to help in teaching someone with dyslexia along with outside sources to use in this endeavor.

~Stacy Matheson, homeschooling parent of a nine-year-old with dyslexia

Unlike any other book I've read on the subject of dyslexia. Beth Ellen Nash shows how to thrive not just survive. So much content!

~Andrea Schattl, homeschooling parent of a child with dyslexia and dysgraphia

My son is a stealth dyslexic who reads well, but spelling and writing are a huge struggle for him...this book gave some great ideas of where to start to remediate as far as the spelling goes!

~Shannon Wagner, homeschooling parent of a 10-year-old with dyslexia

A refreshing resource for educators, special education therapists, medical professionals, parents, and those desiring to learn more about dyslexia. Beth Ellen Nash provides insight and resources for those interacting with dyslexics. She provides encouragement and hope for dyslexics and their families. I highly recommend this book and believe it will make a positive impact on the world dyslexics live in.

~Tammy McGarvey, MSN, RN, FNP-BC, homeschooling parent of children with dyslexia

It is enlightening and refreshing to finally read a book that emphasizes the good points of dyslexia.

~Maria Zarogianni, ESL teacher and parent of a ten-year-old dyslexic, Greece

I found this book extremely helpful! It gave me hope as a homeschool mother and a direction in which to take my children. Many thanks for offering help, hope, and a way forward!

~Homeschooling parent of 12-year-old and seven-year-old girls with dyslexia

Dyslexia
Outside-the-Box

Equipping Dyslexic Kids
to Not Just Survive
but Thrive

Dyslexia
Outside-the-Box

Equipping Dyslexic Kids
to Not Just Survive
but Thrive

Beth Ellen Nash

Dyslexia Outside-the-Box
Equipping Dyslexic Kids to Not Just Survive but Thrive

Published by:
Transformation Books
211 Pauline Drive #513
York, PA 17402
www.TransformationBooks.com

ISBN: 978-1-945252-27-3
Library of Congress Control No: 2017938478

Cover design by: Ranilo Cabo
Layout and typesetting: Ranilo Cabo
Editor: Gwen Hoffnagle
Proofreader: Gwen Hoffnagle
Book Midwife: Carrie Jareed

Printed in the United States of America

Dedication

To all the Hope Academy and Wings to Soar Online Academy students:

While the journey together wasn't always easy,

it was worth it to help you gain your own wings to soar!

I have learned more of what is truly important from working with you

than in any class I ever took.

Table of Contents

Preface

With all the other books out there about dyslexia, why should you read this book? *Dyslexia Outside-the-Box* is the result of my working with dyslexic students of all ages for 17 years. I have sorted through countless strategies that claim to be the "best practice" for supporting struggling students. My personal experiences, both successes and failures, along with the shared experiences of parents who have become comrades, have resulted in transformed lives.

In the introduction I share my story of my hard-won expertise in dyslexia and how I came to establish Wings to Soar Online Academy.

Chapter 1 defines dyslexia by its common characteristics, takes a look at the genetic connection, and reviews some statistics to provide background.

Chapters 2 and 3 redefine dyslexia with a fresh perspective on the strengths of dyslexics – the flip sides of the common challenges – and a whole-person view of dyslexia. Dyslexia is not merely a cluster of weaknesses. The dyslexic has many parallel strengths to be celebrated. There is a flip side to the conventional view of dyslexia as a burden or limitation, and I believe embracing this flip side can be transformational.

Chapters 4, 5, and 6 encourage rethinking learning in the three major academic areas impacted by dyslexia: reading, spelling, and writing.

In Chapter 7 I coin the word *revisioning* as I share Wings to Soar Online Academy's whole-person vision of personalized education, which addresses the unique learning needs of dyslexics.

I purposely placed information that will be valuable to many readers, but would interrupt the flow of the text, in a number of appendices. For some, these appendices will be the most valuable parts of the book and serve as useful references for years to come.

I compiled the most important findings from the extensive reading and training I've done about dyslexia and the most current research on how the brain works. For those of you who wish to read more, I listed the sources I found most helpful in the resources section.

I want to partner with you as you journey on this challenging, but never dull road. My purpose is to provide practical tips, strategies, and direction for remediation that a parent can use at home to help their dyslexic child.

At Wings to Soar our mission is to empower generations of dyslexics to see themselves as uniquely wired. They are not broken, and, like others, they can be successful. They merely need different tools. They have so much to offer the world through their unique flip-side strengths.

There are certainly challenges associated with this particular brain wiring, but I have seen many with dyslexia gain the skills to overcome the challenges and embrace their flip-side dyslexic strengths, providing the confidence to break free from the chains of shame and inadequacy that too often hold back these wonderful individuals. I have had the honor to witness students reach their full potential and become passionate, lifelong learners. Those with dyslexia need not just survive; they can thrive.

I believe this with my whole being, and so do my colleagues at our school. This belief is the bedrock that supports how we teach, learn, and grow at Wings to Soar Online Academy.

Introduction

My name is Beth Ellen Nash. I founded Wings to Soar Online Academy. We create Path to Success™ Personalized Learning Plans for outside-the-box learners at kindergarten through 12th-grade levels. Wings to Soar supports blended learning for our students – a hybrid of homeschool (or afterschool) and online education. I am the individualization and intervention specialist. I am also the curriculum director, in charge of curriculum integration, course creation, and choosing high-quality third-party programs to incorporate into our Path to Success Personalized Learning Plans. Apart from my core Wings to Soar work, I also share my expertise as a speaker, author, consultant, and coach.

I graduated from the School of Education at the University of Wisconsin–Madison in 1998. When we were asked to write our philosophy of education in my first education course, I realized I would need to design my own school someday in order to provide education in the way I believed it needed to be provided.

Even during my student teaching I had a passion for the outside-the-box learner who wasn't making it in the traditional classroom. I asked if I could take a few struggling students to the library to help them with math. I had little experience, but I knew that having these students sit in the back of the classroom completing computation packets because their English skills couldn't keep up with a language-heavy math curriculum was not the solution. We practiced real-world skills like money and measurement. The kids had success! They could learn when they were engaged in meaningful and targeted practice.

I taught in a progressive private school for two years, but left that to gain broader experience toward my goal of starting a school. I spent three years applying for every position I was qualified for that was within an hour of my home. But I believe that I work for the "Divine Placement Agency," and that God closed every door I knocked on for a reason. Had I gotten one of those positions, I know I could have helped a handful of students with their outside-the-box learning needs. However, bureaucratic constraints would have severely limited the scope of what I could truly achieve.

Over this time period I saw that I could have greater impact outside of the traditional classroom. Not knowing yet how that impact should be made, I began tutoring. I learned through trial and error what worked for students facing a variety of challenges. My passion for the struggling learner grew.

I sought additional training as I encountered new learning challenges. I took advanced instruction in attachment disorders, autism, Orton-Gillingham, Davis® Dyslexia Correction, and the National Institute for Learning Development's intervention approaches. Perhaps someday I'll find a university that will allow me to earn a customized master's degree for my hard-won experience and all the additional trainings that don't fit neatly within the current post-bachelor's standards.

Along with tutoring, I was a substitute teacher in classes ranging from kindergarten through 12th grade. During one long-term assignment I was baffled by four students who failed almost every test. I asked for help from another teacher and she told me matter-of-factly, "Some of them just aren't going to make it."

While I said nothing, inside I screamed, "Not on my watch! Not in my classroom!"

"Some of them just aren't going to make it" wasn't an acceptable option. I worked long hours, provided extra help during recess, created curriculum variations to better meet the needs of each student, and designed alternate performance assessments. I also referred students to be evaluated as to whether they qualified to receive special education services. I was so disappointed that the regulations of the public school often prevented the students from getting the help they really needed. I was limited in the help I could offer, and that fact confirmed that I did not belong in a traditional classroom.

A few years later I became a private preschool and kindergarten teacher 10 hours per week for two girls. During that time I also homeschooled a friend's high school freshman, tutored several other students, and taught a science course for a few homeschoolers. Several of these homeschooling families wanted me to provide more structure for their children's academic programs, and shortly thereafter we decided I would be opening a small school. Nine students were enrolled by the time we started six weeks later.

We began with a university-model school, offering in-person classes two days per week and work at home on the other days. The following year we shifted to three days in person and then to four days by the second semester. The next year we moved to full-time classes. Our student population shifted to mostly middle school and high school students who were all struggling learners. I continued with this population, numbering between three to thirteen students each year, for the next five years.

In 2011 I decided that my gifts would better serve a wider audience if I closed the physical school and shifted online. Since then I have offered a hybrid of online education and homeschooling through the online school I founded, Wings to Soar Online Academy. This returned us more closely to our original model of part-time study with a teacher and part-time work at home supervised by the parent. This allows me to reach many more students.

What led to this switch? In over a dozen cities, as I spoke and consulted at homeschool conventions, parents would tell me, "Oh, I wish your school were here!" I realized that with the internet it could be.

As I was sorting out exactly what the online school would look like during the first two pilot years, I had the opportunity to finally get paid for my expertise in reading and language-arts resources. I signed a contract with a charter school to evaluate hundreds of print and online reading and language-arts resources. I sifted out the best of these resources to use at Wings to Soar as well. Parents also recommended several of the quality programs we currently use.

Being trained in the Orton-Gillingham and Davis dyslexia interventions, I spent many years doing phonetic-pattern and word-frequency research to develop a spelling program specifically for my dyslexic students. It only made sense to start targeting dyslexic students as primary pupils for our online school. As I became more and more skilled at creating our Path to Success Personalized Learning Plans for our students through various combinations of programs, I began seeing even better results with students online than I had seen in my one-to-one dyslexia tutoring, and at much lower cost for the families.

Wings to Soar Online Academy is in its sixth year, and in addition to me we have five part-time contract staff members serving more than 120 students in over 20 states and four foreign countries.

I am excited to be able to share with you some of what I have learned over the past 17 years working with dyslexic students. It is my passion to help dyslexics break the chains of shame, failure, and inadequacy that so often surround learning challenges while they learn to see the flip-side strengths of their dyslexia. My mission is to empower dyslexics to become the best versions of themselves, embrace their dyslexia, and gain the skills and confidence to not just survive but thrive in school and in life.

Chapter 1

Defining Dyslexia

In the Genes

There's a saying that goes, "The apple doesn't fall far from the tree." It is very common to find someone in a dyslexic child's parents' or grandparents' generation, and siblings and cousins, who also had or have similar struggles and strengths. According to a study by the Dyslexia Research Trust, at least three genes are linked to dyslexia and "at least ten genetic factors are thought to be involved."[1] Similarly, researchers at the Yale School of Medicine found three genes that predispose individuals to dyslexia and other language impairments.[2] Which genes are involved in any one person gives rise to the variation in how it affects them. If there is one "apple" in the family, it's likely there are more.

"Falling from the same tree" can give the dyslexic child hidden talents. Consider Uncle Stan, who didn't have much time for reading but was a skilled artist with a blowtorch. Or the career of Cousin Samantha, who was slow to read, slow to write, but finished her engineering degree in material science. Shouldn't your nephew Josh be admired for his precocious ability to pilot an airplane before the age of 14 even though he can't spell simple sight words (words children should learn to recognize by sight rather than by sounding them out) or sign his name in cursive? Relatives, siblings, and ancestors who display visual-spatial, mechanical, or technical aspects of thinking are likely the same ones challenged by reading, writing, and arithmetic. In some relatives you might see only the strengths of dyslexia and no particular challenges. Sometimes called *stealth dyslexics*, such people are smart enough to hide their challenges or come up with creative workarounds to overcome them.

What is Dyslexia?

Dyslexia is part of a group of language-based challenges that originate in the brain. This means that the brain struggles to process sounds, recognize words, spell words, and sound out words. Common characteristics of dyslexia include difficulty with:

- Noticing, telling the difference between, and working with the sounds and syllables in oral language (phonological and phonemic awareness)
- Word decoding (sounding out words)
- Fluency in reading, which includes accurate and/or automatic word recognition and an appropriate reading rate for the text type
- Spelling
- Vocabulary
- Comprehension[3]

In order for an official diagnosis of dyslexia to be considered, these challenges can't be due to low intelligence or physical impairments, and the student must be experiencing these challenges in spite of having received effective classroom instruction. (These guidelines were adopted by the International Dyslexia Association Board of Directors on November 12th, 2002. They are also used by the National Institute of Child Health and Human Development (NICHD). Many state education codes, including those of New Jersey, Ohio, and Utah, have adopted these guidelines. Learn more about how consensus was reached on these guidelines at the Definition Consensus Project page at www.dyslexiaida.org.) These characteristics can be detrimental to a child's education without proper intervention, including:

- Loss of desire to read for pleasure or recreation (quite common)
- Limited growth of vocabulary
- Limited acquisition of background knowledge[4]

Early Indicators

The earliest warning signs of dyslexia can include:

- Difficulty rhyming words
- Difficulty learning the alphabet
- Mild speech delays
- Reversing letters and words in reading and writing such as:
  - Reversing letters: "from" instead of "form"
  - Reversing words: "was" instead of "saw"
  - Flipping letters left to right and top to bottom: *b* instead of *d* and *p* instead of *q*
- Being slower at learning to read than one's peers

While mixing up letters and words is what most people associate with dyslexia, reversals are a normal part of development up until first or second grade, particularly in writing. However, these reversals in combination with other dyslexia-related strengths or challenges can be a signal for assessment and early intervention, especially if there is a family history of learning challenges.

Late Bloomers

Many dyslexics tend to learn certain skills later than their peers. This is most typical with language arts, but it can also occur with telling time on an analog clock, telling left from right, and learning rote facts such as times tables.

If in doubt about when to start a dyslexic child in school, waiting a year to allow their brain an additional year to develop is often wise. Once in school, however, it is rarely a good idea to hold a child back, due to the social stigma and negative impact on self-esteem. Exceptions to this are when transitioning between schools at natural breaks (such as middle school to high school, when changing schools, and when transitioning to homeschooling), and in an early grade if they were started in school prior to being developmentally ready.

Early Intervention – Always a Winner

Early intervention prevents unnecessary learning struggles. It minimizes feelings of shame and inadequacy. If there is a family history of dyslexia or other learning challenges, don't assume that a child will "grow out of it."

Choosing to seek a formal diagnosis of dyslexia should be guided by whether or not the student can qualify for *accommodations* (educational strategies that even the playing field for students with dyslexia and other learning challenges) and/or services that might be recommended as a result of that diagnosis. The informal assessments we offer at Wings to Soar are often adequate for finding the "just-right level" a student needs and for starting intervention. In many cases we can help a student get caught up to their age-level skills in one or two years for less than what a formal diagnosis costs. Often the best approach is to use existing financial resources for intensive early intervention, as if the student were dyslexic. If the student needs accommodations to level the playing field on high-stakes tests, then it may be important to get an official diagnosis. If a formal diagnosis is provided when the student is in elementary school, middle school, or early high school, another one will have to be obtained within three years of college entrance to qualify for accommodations at that time.

If the student is not responding well to early intervention after six months despite spending the time according to the protocol for that intervention, it would be wise to seek formal diagnosis to find out if the learning challenge involves other layers of complexity. Addressing the issues early with the help of appropriate professionals minimizes frustrations and damage to the student's self-esteem.

You are the expert on your child – listen to your instincts.

Helpful Statistics

Statistics can be impersonal, but they help reframe the medical/psychological definition of dyslexia into an idea that empowers. Realizing how common dyslexia is and seeing how many other dyslexics have been and are successful in respected fields can reframe it from "something wrong with me" to an experience that many others share.

- Between 6 and 7 percent of US school children have received a diagnosis of an official learning disability. Reading and language processing are the main learning challenges for 85 percent of those kids.[5]
- As many as 15 to 20 percent of the US population has some of the symptoms of dyslexia, including:
  - Slow or inaccurate reading
  - Poor spelling
  - Poor writing
  - Mixing up similar words.[6]
- Eighty to ninety percent of dyslexics have difficulty with phonological processing.[7]
- Over half of dyslexics also have difficulty with procedural processing, including:
  - following the steps of a multi-step math problem
  - the writing process
  - creating a weekly schedule
  - organizing and prioritizing homework[8]

- Thirty-five percent of US entrepreneurs are dyslexic.[9]
- In some colleges the incidence of dyslexia among art and engineering students is more than double the rate of the student body as a whole.[10]
- In his book *Thinking Like Einstein*, Thomas West quotes Massachusetts Institute of Technology (MIT) Media Lab founder and dyslexic Nicholas Negroponte as stating that "dyslexia is so common at MIT that it's locally known as the 'MIT disease.'"[11]

Despite these encouraging statistics, too many kids give up on themselves and quit trying when they don't receive the targeted intervention, support, and accommodations they need during their school years. Teenagers with reading problems are at significantly higher risk for suicide and for dropping out of school than typical readers. A disproportionate number of those with reading struggles end up in prison. Less than one-third of children with reading disabilities are receiving services in their schools to help overcome their reading disabilities. The services that are available rarely include the systematic, direct, explicit multisensory phonetic instruction that dyslexics need. With the appropriate interventions, the cycle of these sad statistics does not need to continue.

There is more good news. Dyslexics have many strengths that can work in their favor when given the right opportunities. Chapters 2 and 3 offer a refreshing, hopeful perspective on these strengths that can help change these statistics for the better.

Chapter 2

Redefining Dyslexia:
A Fresh Look at the Challenges
and the Flip-Side Strengths

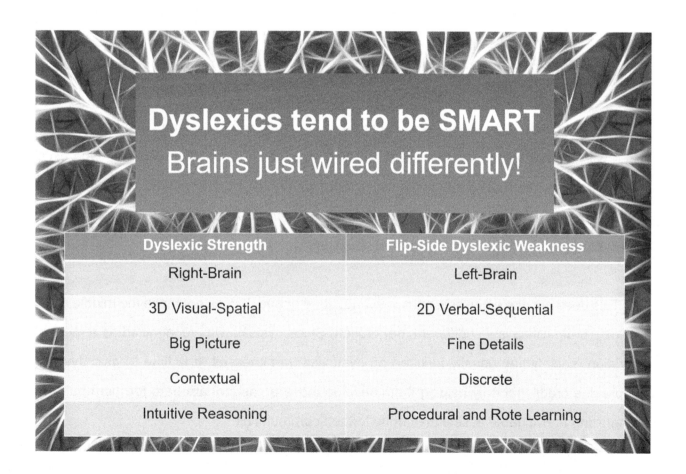

Dyslexics tend to be SMART
Brains just wired differently!

Dyslexic Strength	Flip-Side Dyslexic Weakness
Right-Brain	Left-Brain
3D Visual-Spatial	2D Verbal-Sequential
Big Picture	Fine Details
Contextual	Discrete
Intuitive Reasoning	Procedural and Rote Learning

In this chapter I expand on the strengths discussed in the excellent book *The Dyslexic Advantage,* by Drs. Brock and Fernette Eide. My unique, and I believe powerful contribution is connecting many of the struggles associated with dyslexia with their flip-side strengths. I will address five separate spectrums of learning approaches. Not all of the strengths and weaknesses appear in any given dyslexic to the same degree. This is likely because there are many different genes that contribute to dyslexia as well as different environmental influences. Recognizing that challenges are at the other end of each continuum of related strengths provides a refreshing and encouraging perspective. The charts in the sections below show the strengths of those on each end of the continuums. Following each chart is a discussion of how this often plays out for a dyslexic.

Skills that dyslexics tend to be good at operate on a continuum. An individual with strong three-dimensional picture-thinking skills has a hard time with two-dimensional skills. Those who excel in big-picture thinking tend to have more difficulty with fine, detail-oriented skills, which make up much of reading and math.

Some dyslexics are very weak in some areas and only minimally weak in others. It is the same with the strengths; like any skill or ability, these fall on a continuum. People who excel in one direction have brains that are wired differently from the brains of those who excel in the other. People who are in the middle of the continuum are not as strong in that skill as those at either end, but they don't have the related challenges either.

This does not make one side right or wrong, good or bad. It does not make the middle ideal. Dyslexic brain wiring is just different, not broken. Since dyslexia was recognized as a medical condition, society has usually focused on dyslexics' weaknesses. It is time to give dyslexic people due credit, not only helping them develop those areas that are hard for them but also recognizing the valuable assets they bring to their communities.

There are several distinct strengths of dyslexics, and there are subtle differences in how their weaknesses play out, especially in the final three continuums discussed below. All of these are best addressed through direct instruction that breaks apart the separate skills and explicitly teaches them in the sequential order needed.

Right-Brain versus Left-Brain

Dyslexics show greater strength with right-brain functions than with left-brain functions. In his book *In the Mind's Eye*, Thomas West suggests thinking patterns that favor use of the right side of the brain, which is directly related to visual, spatial, and other talents seen in many dyslexics.[1] Viewing dyslexia through the strengths that the right-brain functions have to offer is empowering.

Technology has allowed researchers to look into the brain via functional magnetic resonance imaging (fMRI). Findings show that specific areas in the left sides of the brains of typical readers are engaged when they read fluently. Using fMRI, Yale researchers Drs. Sally and Bennett Shaywitz first demonstrated that while reading, the right hemisphere of the brain is activated in dyslexics more than the left hemisphere, which is usually more dominant for reading[2] and shows more scattered activity in general.[3] Patterns of activation for language processing that typically occur in the right hemisphere of the dyslexic brain are broader, slower, but much richer than left-hemisphere-dominated processing.[4]

Many of the strengths associated with dyslexia seem to be directly connected to a right-brain-dominant learning style, while their weaknesses are in areas in which the left brain is more dominant.

Right-Brain Dominant	Left-Brain Dominant
• Nonverbal information	• Spoken and written language
• Drawing	• Sequencing
• Construction	• Word analysis
• Creative	• Numbers
• Intuitive	• Letters
• Spatial relationships	• Analytical
	• Logical[5]

The effects of these differences are discussed following each of the charts below that go into more depth on these aspects of right-brain and left-brain thinking styles.

3-D Visual-Spatial versus 2-D Verbal-Sequential

Two-dimensional thinking is a part of verbal-sequential thinking and is linear and sequential in nature. Those with visual-spatial strengths have three-dimensional thinking styles that connect everything into a whole that is perceived simultaneously from multiple perspectives. Many dyslexics have incredible three-dimensional (3-D) thinking, which contributes to visual-spatial strengths. Their weakness in two-dimensional (2-D), linear, sequential skills is a direct tradeoff for these flip-side strengths.

3-D Visual-Spatial	2-D Verbal-Sequential
(Dyslexic Flip-Side Strengths)	(Dyslexic Weaknesses)
• Thinks in pictures, creating an ongoing 3-D movie of connected images in the mind	• Thinks in words rather than pictures, with internal dialogue
• Plays the movie in the mind, visualizing the interactions and reactions of events and people to one another	• Linear thought follows the structure of language
• Quickly synthesizes new data, and views the "scene" from many different angles and perspectives	• Mentally composes sentences, one word at a time, at about the same speed as speech[8]
• Understands visual-spatial features including shape, size, motion, position, and orientation of physical objects.[6]	• 2-D
• Likes diagrams	• Sequential
• Learns well from practical demonstrations	• Logical
• Thinks in terms of systems rather than discrete objects	• Likes protocols and standard operating procedures[9]
• Good at breaking things apart and putting them back together[7]	

Brains that think in 3-D don't intuitively know what to do with flat, ordered bits of information. Words like *was* and *saw* look the same. When 3-D thinkers try to approach 2-D symbols (words, numbers, and musical notation), their thoughts become disconnected. To maneuver in a 2-D world requires that things like reading, spelling, writing, and some types of math be done in a sequential, linear fashion.[10] Is it any wonder that a dyslexic has difficulty getting the vivid 3-D movie in their brain onto the page when they try to write? They are having to use a much slower sequential and verbal approach that is at the opposite end of the spectrum from what their brains are wired to do so well.

It's easy to understand why reversals are a common symptom among dyslexics once you realize that their brains are wired to process well in three dimensions. Depending on where they are viewed from, the letters *b*, *p*, *d*, and *q* are all the same.[11]

Bringing to mind nouns and verbs is easy for the visual-spatial thinker due to their ability to associate images such as "apple" and "running" with the corresponding words. Most of the little connector words simply do not have an image to associate with them. The dyslexic mind cannot make sense of these words and may skip over them entirely even though they make up a high percentage of the most commonly used words in English. All of the first 13 words in frequency of usage, which make up 25 percent of written English, are these non-picturable words. Two hundred more such words add another significant percentage. This is partially why dyslexics comprehend far better when they read silently than when they have to read aloud, as they can get the gist even when skipping over these many non-picturable words.[12]

Just because dyslexics tend to be stronger in visual-spatial thinking than someone who is not dyslexic does not mean that they cannot improve, or even master, 2-D skills. Imagine the tremendous potential and creativity of a dyslexic who has been equipped to use their natural 3-D thinking as well as having been trained to work in the 2-D world!

See appendix A for more detail on the Davis Dyslexia Correction method, which teaches a mental tool that allows the dyslexic to consciously choose to temporarily turn off their intuitive 3-D thinking when they want to work in 2-D mode.

Big Picture versus Fine Detail

Neuroscience has identified other differences in the brains of dyslexics besides being right-brain dominant. Dr. Manuel Casanova of the University of Kentucky School of Medicine studied spacing differences in the minicolumns of the cortex, or outer layer of the brain. Differences in the spacing appear to be connected to different processing strengths. The minicolumns in dyslexic brains are more widely spaced than in those of non-dyslexics. This corresponds with the associated strength in big-picture thinking, along with the flip-side weakness in fine detail.[13]

Big Picture	**Fine Details**
(Dyslexic Flip-Side Strengths)	(Dyslexic Weaknesses)
• Sees the big picture	• Focuses in on one thing at a time
• Sees from multiple perspectives	• Notices nuances
• Makes connections[14]	• Sees shades of meaning
• Brings information, processes, and strategies from different disciplines to bear on an issue	• Picks up patterns subconsciously
• Sees similarities, associations, correlations, and cause and effect between ideas, objects, concepts, and points of view[15]	• Examples of details are borrowing and carrying numbers, memorizing math facts, and distinguishing small differences in sounds and words[16]

Kids with dyslexia tend to struggle a lot in early grades because there is so much detail work expected in these foundational years. Most dyslexics have difficulty learning the symbols that correspond with the sounds in our language, and benefit from intensive instruction in phonics. Dyslexics tend not to discover the rules and patterns of all the individual bits of information on their own. They need direct, systematic, sequential, explicit instruction with plenty of practice to master these discrete bits of information.[17] This is addressed in more detail in chapter 4 and in appendix A.

As children move into high school and college, their schools begin to value making connections, analogies, and inferences. Dyslexics are good at these. Schools and parents need to get students past the foundational skills which I describe in more detail in later chapters. Then a dyslexic student can shine in big-picture thinking. Many dyslexics come into their own academically once they get past introductory-level college courses and start studying areas of interest to them. It is here where strong big-picture thinking is highly valued.

Dyslexics are good at taking multiple perspectives into account during conversations and when solving problems.[18] They do well in interdisciplinary studies in which their strength in interconnected thinking is valued. They often make very mature and sophisticated connections. In the face of decoding challenges, dyslexics' abilities to use context and background knowledge help reading comprehension.[19]

All students benefit from making as many connections as they can between ideas they are learning in school and the rest of what they know. The brain stores and retrieves information better when varied and meaningful connections are made while learning. For dyslexics with contextual learning strengths, creating associations across multiple subjects is natural and essential.

At Wings to Soar Online Academy, we do just that in our Integrated Liberal Studies (ILS) courses. These courses play to a dyslexic's strengths and create rich connections for all, dyslexic or not. We weave the following topics into a four-year curriculum with history at its core:

- Literature and composition
- Art and music appreciation
- Government and economics

- Geography
- Philosophy and religion
- Science and technological developments

Contextual versus Discrete

Dyslexic brains are not wired to process discrete bits of information well. This is information that is isolated and out of context, such as a list of dates or events. On the flip-side, many dyslexics have strong contextual skills that allow them to process information well when learned through stories, simulations, illustrations, examples, and case studies.

Contextual (Dyslexic Flip-Side Strengths)	Discrete (Dyslexic Weaknesses)
• Connects otherwise discrete information through associated examples, stories, or illustrations • Mentally constructs or re-creates a series of episodes or scenes • Uses episodic memory to reconstruct past trends • Projects forward to solve future problems • Tests scenarios in the mind to foreshadow outcomes of a proposed idea or course of action • Are skilled storytellers (and possibly skilled at creative writing)[20]	• Memorizes isolated pieces of information • Learns naturally by breaking down information into individual steps and subcomponents and then putting it back together as a whole • Isolates and recombines individual segments of skills being learned, such as spelling patterns and math facts

When encouraged to use examples and illustrations rather than relying on abstract concepts and definitions, narrative thinkers make deeper, broader connections, and they reason, learn, and remember more effectively. Dyslexics with contextual thinking strengths often learn history better through historical fiction and documentaries.

Discrete skills, such as writing letters, sounding out words, and distinguishing spelling patterns, rely on repetition or memorization of seemingly unrelated tasks and bits of information that are not integrated until months or even years later. This is why it's so important to explicitly teach the rules, patterns, and generalizations. Dyslexics need to understand what they're learning, not just memorize disconnected bits of data.

Dyslexic brains are not wired to process abstract (non-picturable) information well. Dyslexic learners especially need to understand why and how new knowledge connects to what they already know. They also want to know how it is relevant to their lives. "Memorize this because the teacher said so" or "because you're going to need it someday" doesn't work for dyslexics – and rarely works for anyone else either. While the desire to please is earnest, a dyslexic brain just isn't wired for that kind of learning.

Quality documentary films build rich vocabulary and background knowledge by making use of both visual and auditory learning strengths in a narrative format that dyslexics often find engaging. Reading or listening to a passage that connects to a topic in which a dyslexic has built a substantial amount of background knowledge through such audio-visual resources enables dyslexics to use their strength of contextual reasoning as they read.

Intuitive Reasoning versus Procedural and Rote Learning

Intuitive reasoners consciously, or often subconsciously, take in a body of information and come to conclusions about it. Intuitive reasoners, using dynamic, real-world reasoning, often can't tell you how they came to their conclusions – they just know.

Procedural learning involves the steps needed to complete a task. Rote learning is memorization of information merely by repetition and practice, as opposed to being based on a deep understanding of the concept. About half of dyslexics have difficulty with procedural learning and many more have difficulty with rote learning.

Intuitive Reasoning (Dyslexic Flip-Side Strength)	Procedural and Rote Learning (Dyslexic Weaknesses)
• Discerns patterns and trends in the real world • Quick processing • Predicts likely outcomes, even with limited information, by playing out many possibilities and scenarios in their head • Excels with unknown or changing variables[21]	• Learns and follows steps of a procedure • Memorizes well • Can spit back the expected facts on demand • Does well when the information to be learned is clearly defined • Meticulous

Dyslexics process real-world situations very quickly because they excel at looking at the big picture. The downside to fast, intuitive processing is the marked contrast of the dyslexic's slow verbal-processing speed.

The brain of the intuitive processor works so quickly that the tongue cannot keep up. Their relatively slower verbal-processing speed leaves observers with the impression they are stupid, daydreaming, not paying attention, or lazy.[22]

To the surprise of many math teachers, intuitive processors are usually correct in their conclusions even though they can't re-create the steps they went through mentally to reach their conclusions. They are often scolded for not showing their work.

The purpose of having students show their steps is to allow the teacher to detect and correct errors. If errors do not exist, teachers and parents should not frustrate dyslexics by insisting on explanations that are not readily available. If they can explain their thinking, enjoy the insight into the unique way the student thinks. If it makes sense to them and it works, this process is likely more effective for them than following steps they do not understand.

If following specific steps in a procedure or task is truly important, dyslexics need explicit instruction and practice in how to carry out the required steps. Dyslexic brains do not usually excel at rote learning.

Einstein said it was difficult to put into words the complex ideas he had in his head. He understood what was in his head, but explaining it to someone else, especially in writing, was very difficult. In spite of this challenge he published 20 academic papers, including his theory of relativity, in 1905 alone.

Ron Davis, author of *The Gift of Dyslexia* and *The Gift of Learning*, refers to dyslexia as the "gift of mastery." While it can take a dyslexic more repetition and review in process-based and rote-based learning, once they understand a concept they've truly mastered it and you can't take it away from them.[23]

Teaching Ideas

By making the most of the strengths of a dyslexic-wired brain and tailoring learning to these strengths, learning does not need to be so difficult. Present content by:

- Transforming abstract information into narrative or visual form
- Using examples, illustrations, simulations, stories, narratives, and case studies
- Asking questions that facilitate understanding, such as:
  - Calling attention to fine details that big-picture thinkers might not notice
  - Helping sort out the main idea from the supporting details
  - Reminding students of related things they already know and to which they can connect new information
  - Introducing analogies
  - Triggering reasoning in directions not yet explored

Here are a few examples of improved learning experiences that tap in to dyslexic strengths to help make learning much more memorable:

- Have the student pretend to be a blood cell traveling through the circulatory system, or part of the immune system attacking a germ invading a cell.
- A number of challenging physics concepts, including the theory of relativity, are made understandable, at even a middle school level, by teaching the concepts through story, as in the *Uncle Albert* books by Russell Stannard.
- Having the student imagine themselves in a far off time or place experiencing a historic event or another culture, or even reenacting it, can help integrate and cement otherwise isolated facts.
  - Historical fiction books and documentaries are great for doing this.
  - The student can create their own short story verbally or in writing. Putting themselves into the setting helps them more fully engage and make use of narrative-reasoning strengths.

- Help the student create metaphors between something familiar and what they are trying to learn. "How was ___ like ___?" or "What is ___ similar to?" can tie things together. It is best if they can make the connection themselves rather than your saying, "That's like___." If you need to do that to get the thoughts flowing, then ask, "What else is it like?"

  For example, reflecting on the question "How were the years leading up to the French Revolution like the buildup to a thunderstorm?" gets at the major events leading up to the Revolution and also helps them understand the significance at a deeper level.

- Create mnemonic memory devices to help the student learn a series of facts, such as HOMES for remembering the five Great Lakes: Huron, Ontario, Michigan, Erie, and Superior. A new mnemonic sentence to remember the planets (without the dwarf planets) is "My Very Excellent Mother Just Served Us Nachos."

- Challenge the student to create interesting stories using only the words they have learned so far. An artistic student might want to use their spelling words as doodles from which they create pictures. Be sure to have them see and say the word, then spell it, and then repeat the word so they get these multisensory inputs as well as their creative one. Do this before and after the drawing.

- Use the letters of the word they are spelling as the first letters of the words in a sentence for which the word can serve as a helpful mnemonic reinforcer. It is best if the mnemonic sentence has some relation to the word, but not essential. Silly sentences are easier to remember. Since the sentence is pictorial, the words in the sentence do not need to be limited to ones they have learned to read or spell.

- Coming up with stories or illustrations that incorporate a math fact the student is having trouble learning is another way to use their dyslexic strengths. For example, you have to be 16 to drive a 4x4 pickup truck. Another example is that 1, 2, 3, 4 can help recall 12 = 3 x 4. The challenge to remember 7 x 8 becomes much easier with 5, 6, 7, 8, triggering 56 = 7 x 8.

- Setting information to be learned to catchy tunes like "Three Blind Mice," "Twinkle, Twinkle Little Star," or "Happy Birthday" can be an excellent aid. One idea for this is to learn to skip-count by 3s to the tune of "Jingle Bells":

3, 6, 9	(Jingle bells)
12, 15	(jingle bells)
18, 21	(jingle all the way)
24	(oh what fun)
27	(it is to ride)
...30 and now you're done!	(in a one-horse open sleigh)

Have fun as you and your child come up with many more creative ways to make learning enjoyable and tap in to their dyslexic flip-side strengths. I invite you to share your creative ideas for stories and mnemonic devices to aid in memorization in the Dyslexia Outside-the-Box Facebook group. Ask for suggestions from others in the group if they are not already there.

The weaknesses dyslexics commonly experience are directly related to their flip-side strengths. Their brains are just wired differently. The goal should not be to find a cure but to help them become the highest functioning dyslexics they can be. This includes using teaching strategies that tap in to their strengths, acknowledging and addressing the associated weaknesses, and helping them learn some of the foundational reading, spelling, and writing skills, which I address in chapters 4, 5, and 6.

Chapter 3

Redefining Dyslexia: A Whole-Person View

In *The Dyslexia Empowerment Plan,* Ben Foss, a dyslexic with dual law and MBA degrees, brings much needed relief. To paraphrase one of his core messages: I have good news for you. You can't cure dyslexia because it's not a disease. Dyslexics aren't broken so you can't fix them. Their brains are just different.[1]

Flip-Side-Strenths Perspective versus Deficits Perspective

Think of dyslexia as a way of thinking, or a processing style. Many of the challenges of dyslexia are direct trade-offs for flip-side strengths, as we explored in the last chapter. These strengths typically go unrecognized.

Consider the differences between the two sides of the chart on the following page – flip-side strengths on the left compared to deficits on the right.

Flip-Side-Strengths Perspective[2]	Deficits Perspective[3]
• Good problem solvers • Creative • Observant • Strong social skills and high levels of empathy • Excellent big-picture thinkers • Good at making connections • Three-dimensional thinking • Strong narrative reasoning	• Inaccurate and/or non-fluent word recognition • Poor spelling and decoding abilities • Difficulty with organization of sounds to process language • Slow or inaccurate reading, including mixing up similar words • Poor written composition • Difficulty understanding math word problems

Be the First to Erase Stereotypes and Embrace Dyslexia

A stigma surrounds people with dyslexia. That stigma is often unwittingly reinforced by family members. Parents who are still coming to grips with their child's differences may feel they can't talk to others about it. Who would understand? Because of the negative labels society uses, parents sometimes refuse to have this difference properly identified; they don't want their child to know they're different. But a dyslexic kid already knows they're different. They have been wondering, perhaps longer than their parents, "What's wrong with me?"

Give it a name. Help them accept who they are – not just in part, but as a whole person. Dyslexia should not define them entirely, but naming it helps them accept that part of them.

Unfortunately, being different can be perceived as a bad thing. Parents should affirm the strengths their child has and communicate that these are the flip-sides of the struggles. If parents help youngsters understand the flip-side strengths that go along with the challenges, both can begin to embrace dyslexia.

Dyslexics are often wrongly perceived as being lazy or unmotivated because their difficulties are in direct contrast with their other amazing abilities. It is easy to see why a dyslexic person gives up in despair when previous efforts at making sense of their differences are met with indifference and/or silence from those in a position to help. In the end it's easier to accept "I didn't do well because I didn't really try" than "I must be stupid; I tried very hard, but still didn't succeed." A diminished sense of self-worth sets in, caused by the excessive struggle to learn without results. A downward emotional spiral begins. But dyslexics actually work much harder than non-dyslexics to achieve the same level of academic learning mastery in a system that focuses heavily on reading; writing; and linear, step-by-step work.

Helping dyslexics embrace their strengths allows them to gain the resiliency to bounce back from the challenges of life. Tools such as ear-reading (listening to text rather than reading it), speech-to-text, predictive text, spell check, grammar check, and calculators can shore up their weaknesses so they can better succeed with their strengths. I talk about these tools for leveling the playing field in appendix B.

Dyslexics can tell that learning is harder for them than for others. They need acceptance and support from teachers, friends, and family throughout their entire lives. A balanced perspective that addresses both strengths and weaknesses can make all the difference. Help a dyslexic understand what it is they're dealing with, but redefine dyslexia as a positive, powerful difference. If parents lead by example, identifying flip-side strengths that go along with the challenges, dyslexic kids can learn to embrace their unique wiring.

An eight-year-old boy came up to me after a talk I gave on the flip-side strengths and challenges of dyslexia, and with a smile on his face told me, "You were totally describing me!" Finally he had a name for what was different about him and was able to embrace it.

Society has taught that the future prospects of dyslexics are limited. But they are capable and skilled in different ways from those of much of the rest of the population. Whether or not they pursue higher education, they do not need to settle for low-paying dead-end jobs. They can graduate from college or a technical school (if this fits with their interests and skills) when provided the appropriate support. Through hard work, perseverance, and the right tools they can excel in many careers. Solutions for many of the world's problems will likely be discovered by these bright, observant, "different" kids! History is full of dyslexic role models who changed the face of society because of their "difference."

Dyslexic Greats

Throughout history dyslexics have been highly valued, not because of their deficits, but because of their flip-side strengths. Thomas West's book *In The Mind's Eye: Creative Visual Thinkers, Gifted Dyslexics, and the Rise of Visual Technologies* might have a cumbersome title, but it is a must-read for parents of dyslexics and adults with dyslexia. West's book introduces the reader to "eleven remarkable people: three physicists, two mathematicians, two inventors, an artist, a political leader, a military leader, and a poet." It portrays people who changed the world at least in part because of their dyslexic strengths. It is surprising who they were!

- Born September 22nd, 1791, this physicist had "early problems with speech and some notable deficiencies in spelling, punctuation and capitalization...His greatest difficulties were problems with mathematics and an unreliable memory." Several of his positive traits that are common flip-side dyslexic strengths include "a powerful imagination...a strong predisposition to look at the whole rather than the parts...a fierce originality of thought and approach." This remarkable man created spatial models two centuries before computer modeling was used. Though he could not prove some of his theories during his lifetime, his work "provided a set of utterly original mathematical concepts which...brought mathematics to the center of a new kind of physics in the next century." He has a law of electromagnetic induction named after him, his very own mathematical constant, and he coined the words *electrode*, *cathode*, and *ion*. You might remember him from physics class. His name? Michael Faraday.

- This inventor's work is directly responsible for entertainment icons like Elizabeth Taylor, Mickey Mouse, and Justin Bieber. In addition to being sickly and hearing-impaired, he shared that "father thought [I] was stupid, and I almost decided I must be a dunce." He had a poor memory and terrible writing mechanics, but a powerful ability to easily make "connections between distant and apparently unrelated entities." A contemporary of fellow dyslexic Nikola Tesla, this gentleman is known worldwide as Thomas Alva Edison.

- This politician and his creative, unorthodox methods would change the lives of people worldwide in the 20th century. He "was a failure at school (last in his class)," and had a speech impediment that stayed with him his entire life. He was "erratic, unpredictable, [at times] frightening," and, as quoted by West, "a man with 'a zigzag streak of lightning in the brain.'" This gentleman was easily distracted, chronically late, struggled with arithmetic and reading, never improvised a speech, and "had a great deal of difficulty with words." Yet he became one of the most "prominent and widely respected world leaders during a period of pivotal conflict...a hero." His leadership, "masterful skills as an orator," and "unusual energy and vision" secure his place in history as Great Britain's greatest prime minister, Winston Churchill.

- This famous dyslexic also had attention deficit disorder (ADD), and in 1972 the publisher of his personal papers was forced to preface the collection with a note to readers that "while every effort has been made to preserve the flavor of...spelling and punctuation...in [many cases] periods, and capital letters have been added to help the reader." Though dyslexia and ADD were not understood until decades afterward, this man's parents "enveloped him in affection [though]...hardly comprehending his strange affliction." He struggled with pronunciation, penmanship, spelling, and reading, and was accident prone. West goes on to say that though "he showed many signs of... dyslexia when young...[many] residual traits were evident for the rest of his life." His gift of a global view as applied to historic, mechanical, and technical achievements was instrumental in his successfully commanding divisions of soldiers during World War II. His abilities in spatial relationships were significant to "his acknowledged skill in command." He received the Purple Heart, the Bronze Star, the Distinguished Service Cross, the Legion of Merit, and the Distinguished Service Medal while in the military. He will forever be remembered by a single moniker: Patton.[4]

These four men, along with Da Vinci, Yeats, Einstein, Tesla, Dodgson, Poincaré, and Maxwell, make up a diverse list of dyslexic great men who forever changed the world, according to West.

The past is not the only place to look for dyslexic world-changers. There are many famous and successful modern-day dyslexics: Whoopi Goldberg (actress, comedian), Jay Leno (talk show host), Henry Winkler (actor, director, producer, writer), Orlando Bloom (actor), Charles Schwab (businessman), Jack Horner (journalist), Steven Spielberg (director), Sir Richard Branson (business magnate, investor, philanthropist), and Steve Jobs (Apple computer founder), to name a few. Dyslexics are capable of excelling as skilled laborers, researchers, entrepreneurs, entertainers, scientists, teachers, leaders, and other world-changers.

Obtain a copy of *In the Mind's Eye* and seek out other stories of dyslexics whose powerful flip-side strengths helped them succeed in spite of, or more likely because of, their dyslexia.

As you can see from the examples of famous dyslexics above, many thrive in careers in which they step outside the box. For many dyslexics it is preferable to become an entrepreneur doing something they are good at than to be a square peg in a round hole at some job. They are usually most successful when they surround themselves with people who are strong in their weak areas. Ideally everyone should spend 85 percent of their time doing what they do best, and hire out the rest.[5]

Be the first to embrace dyslexia.

Accept dyslexia in your loved one as you would accept a musical talent, a sense of style, or the ability to bake bread. Be the one to unmask the flip-side strengths.

You're not going to cure dyslexia. You can help the dyslexics in your life gain some eye-reading skills, you can help them get their thoughts on paper in a more standard format, but you're not going to cure dyslexia. In fact, you wouldn't want to. Many of the qualities you love and adore about the dyslexics in your life probably include parts that are wired in – the trade-offs for things that are tripping them up.

Their diagnoses only partially describe them. The more traditional understanding of dyslexia does not highlight their strengths. It should not define them. Help them see that, like everyone else, they are individuals with strengths and weaknesses. Consistently express the fact that you value them as whole people, including both their weaknesses and strengths. This can easily get overlooked when struggling to cope with the weaknesses.

I hope this strengths perspective helps you adopt an alternate viewpoint. I hope it frees you to let go of needing to find a cure. The goal should be to help dyslexics become the highest-functioning people they can be. This includes helping them learn some of the foundational reading, spelling, and writing skills that I address in chapters 4, 5, and 6.

Chapter 4

Rethinking Learning – Reading

The National Reading Panel reviewed more than 100,000 reading studies and identified five skills essential for reading success: phonological and phonemic awareness, phonics, fluency, vocabulary, and reading comprehension. This massive study concluded in 2000, and the resulting report has guided the development of reading programs ever since.[1] The following are strategies and programs that Wings to Soar has found helpful in strengthening each of these areas.

Phonological and Phonemic Awareness

While the terms *phonological awareness* and *phonemic awareness* are often used interchangeably, phonemic awareness really is a subset of phonological awareness. Tasks that work on phonological and phonemic awareness are oral and do not include working with the symbols of print.[2] (I address *phonics*, which involves the relationship between sounds and associated written symbols, in the next section.) K12Reader, an online reading instruction resource, tells us:

> Phonological awareness is the ability to recognize that words are made up of a
> variety of sound units...A child with strong phonological awareness should be
> able to recognize and use rhyme, break words into syllables, blend phonemes

into syllables and words, identify the beginning and ending sounds in a syllable and see smaller words within larger words (i.e. "cat" in "catalog").[3]

Phonemic awareness involves only the phoneme, which is the smallest unit of sound:

A reader with strong phonemic awareness will demonstrate the ability to hear rhyme and alliteration (the repetition of the same consonant sound at the beginning of several different words used in a sentence or paragraph), find the different sound in a set of words (i.e. "bat", "ball", "wet") and blend and segment phonemes.[4]

Phonological and phonemic awareness lay an important foundation for later reading success. Being able to identify, distinguish between, and manipulate individual sounds is especially important in spelling. Dyslexics can have difficulty making the connection between a visual symbol (a letter) for an auditory experience (a sound), which is phonics, and is addressed in the next section.

Difficulty rhyming words (such as *bat*, *cat*, and *hat*) is a common early indication of dyslexia. Not distinguishing between similar sounds (such as /d/ and /t/) at the beginning, middle, or end of a word is another example of struggles with phonological awareness. (Forward-slashes on either side of letters indicate that you should read or say the *sound* of the letter(s) rather than the name(s) of the letters.) A student with this challenge would have trouble when asked to use colored blocks to show the change from *had* to *hat* by replacing the block where they heard the different sound with a different-colored block. If they can't hear the difference between similar sounds, they might try to spell *chug* and it comes out *jug* instead. If they can distinguish between the sounds but are having difficulty with only the pronunciation of the similar sounds, that can indicate speech articulation issues.

A student having difficulty with phonological and phonemic awareness should begin with a program that starts at the sound level before moving on to phonics, which is sound-symbol association. Some dyslexics, and most individuals with *auditory processing disorder*, need to start here in order for the phonics-based instruction to be effective.

Resources for Developing Phonological and Phonemic Awareness

Please see appendix F where I provide a series of phonological and phonemic awareness exercises to use with your child to strengthen these skills. The drills can also serve as informal assessment tools to determine whether or not a child is struggling in this area. Using these exercises to practice phonological-awareness skills and phonemic-awareness skills can be adequate for some to address the challenge. Others might need more intensive intervention.

If the phonological-processing problem persists after working on these exercises, it may be that the child has auditory-processing challenges and will need more intensive intervention. A full evaluation by an audiologist as suggested in appendix G is the only way to diagnose auditory processing disorder. Difficulties with phonological processing are usually part of auditory-processing challenges, but auditory processing disorder affects many other areas as well.

Other resources that parents and tutors can use to strengthen phonological and phonemic awareness:

- *Literacy Leaders* is a book from Educators Publishing Service that has many exercises with prepared word lists to use with a child with mild challenges in this area.
- The Lindamood-Bell LiPS® program begins at this sound-discrimination level. It draws attention to the shape the mouth makes with each different sound, where the sound is made in the mouth, and how it feels to make the sound. While this program is highly effective, it needs to be conducted by a licensed practitioner, and can be fairly expensive.

- At Wings to Soar we've found that one of the most effective programs for treating a persistent phonological-processing challenge is Fast ForWord®. In addition to targeted exercises to help with phonological-processing challenges and auditory-processing challenges, this well-researched program begins by focusing on the underlying cognitive functions of memory, attention, processing speed, and sequencing, which provide the groundwork for all reading skills. Only then does the program move on to address reading directly.

Phonics

One of the common struggles for dyslexic kids is that they have difficulty sounding out new words. Knowing which letter symbol(s) go with which sounds is what phonics is all about. Difficulties with phonics affect both reading and spelling. Most students benefit from learning the most common sound-symbol pairings for spelling, if nothing else.

Because English draws from so many languages, there are more possible sound-symbol pairings for each sound than in most other languages. Depending on which researcher one consults, between 80 and 97 percent of English words do follow phonetic patterns. The question is whether any given phonetic pattern occurs in words that are common enough to be worth teaching. The top 1,000 most frequently used words make up 90 percent of written English, and the top 3,000 make up 97 percent. The dyslexic student should focus on learning patterns that are common in these high-utility words rather than on less common phonetic patterns. I spent many years researching word frequency and have summarized the highest-utility patterns worth learning in appendix E.

Dyslexia results from "a deficit in the phonological component of language" for 80 to 90 percent of dyslexics.[5] For most dyslexics, an Orton-Gillingham phonics-based approach is essential in filling that gap. It may not be the only method needed, especially if the individual has underlying auditory-processing challenges or weakness with phonological awareness.

Many Orton-Gillingham-based programs start at the sound-symbol connection level, but some students need to start further back with underlying cognitive skills (mental-processing skills) or phonological awareness before they can tackle phonics.

Resources for Building Phonics

- Please see the extensive section on the Orton-Gillingham approach, which is considered the gold standard in phonics-based dyslexia intervention, in appendix A about dyslexia intervention options.
- See appendix E for high-frequency phonetic spelling patterns worth learning.

Fluency

Fluency involves the ability to quickly sound out or automatically recognize words by sight at an appropriate pace for the type of reading being done. Fiction can usually be read faster than nonfiction informational text. More difficult text that contains many specialized terms needs to be read more slowly for full comprehension. An appropriate pace for reading a short story is different from that for reading an essay, a poem, a play, or a textbook.

Reading fluency includes reading smoothly and with good expression. This is essential for reading aloud, but also carries over into the phrasing and pace of silent reading. Reading with natural expression and pacing often indicates that the reader is fully comprehending the text; but many dyslexics are much better silent readers than they are at reading aloud, so this definitely should not be seen as the only indicator.

There are other causes for fluency difficulty besides dyslexia. One physical cause can be weak ocular muscles. There are six muscles that control eye movement. A person might notice temporary difficulty with visual tracking after reading for a long period of time. Eye muscles can become fatigued. While this is a normal experience, a developmental optometrist or ophthalmologist can help identify whether or not vision therapy is needed. Programs that help build visual-tracking efficiency can also help if this is the cause of a student's reading not being fluent. Refer to appendix G where this is discussed in greater depth if concerns in this area are suspected.

Even after dyslexic students have done extensive, explicit work to build their phonics skills, most still need additional targeted work to build up their fluency. They are able to read, but it is painfully slow for the level at which they should be. It is not uncommon for a dyslexic middle school student to have a silent reading rate of a first or second grader. Some approaches that parents and tutors can use to help improve fluency include:

- Employing the "five fingers down" strategy. When the student is reading, they put a finger down for each word they either don't know or have difficulty sounding out. If they put five fingers down before they reach the end of the page, that book is too challenging for fluency practice. There is a time for stretching students to learn new reading skills and tackle more complex text, but it should not be while trying to work on building fluency or enjoyment of reading.

- Engaging student interest. It's important to keep struggling readers engrossed. Reading about topics that they want to learn about or already have background knowledge in can provide context and vocabulary support.

- Making sure the author's style fits the student. Usually within about two to four pages the student knows whether or not they like the author's style. When reading academic content there may be no choice, but when reading to develop fluency, do not force them to read a style or content that turns them off.

Additional suggestions to foster fluency include:

- Reading the material aloud to the student before they read it themselves

- Providing a summary or overview of a long passage so they have an idea of what's coming and can tie it in to their background knowledge

- Previewing vocabulary for them if there are names of places, people, or other vocabulary words they may not know

The goal of fluency practice is to build quick and accurate sight-word recognition. Using a variety of the following types of practices in short sessions works the best with most dyslexic students:

- Have the student listen to a quality model of the passage being read aloud. Then have them read the passage at least two or three times themselves. The goal is to become more fluent each time they read.

- Have the student read along with quality audio or a fluent reader to gain experience with the prosody (the rhythm and musicality) of the language. The audio provides confidence-building support for words they are unsure of.

- Sight-word flashcards build sight-word recognition. Flashcards can be creatively incorporated into games, puzzles, or other activities to make the practice more enjoyable.

- Clay modeling: The Davis Symbol Mastery suggested by the Davis Dyslexia Correction approach helps build sight-word recognition specifically for words that frequently confuse the dyslexic student. Appendix A explains the Davis method in detail.

- The Davis Sweep-Sweep-Spell strategy has the student cover up all but the single word that they're about to read. One by one they uncover each word as they read. If they cannot read a word, they spell it one letter at a time. If they still don't get it, the adult who's reading with them immediately feeds them the word. This builds recognition of the letters of the word from left to right as they come in sequence. This kind of practice should only be done for five to ten minutes at a time. Use text at a level at which the student knows at least 90 percent of the words when working to build up their sight-word recognition.[6]

Resources for Developing Fluency

At Wings to Soar Online Academy we use MindPlay® and Reading Plus® to help build fluency. Reading Plus more specifically includes iBalance exercises to improve efficiency of eye movements, which effectively helps students who have either completed vision therapy or who have only minor visual-tracking issues. Reading Plus works equally well for dyslexics and others who have learned the foundational phonics skills but are just reading slowly and/or having difficulty with comprehension. MindPlay helps fill in phonetic skill gaps, as well as build fluency.

Resources for building sight words, which helps build fluency, include:

- The Nessy™ online reading and spelling program, which incorporates fun animations with mnemonics, helps some students remember sight words. (This is one of the programs we often use at Wings to Soar.)

- Diane Craft's Right Brain Dolch Sight Word Cards, Lone Star Learning®, and SnapWords®, which all have visual sight-word cards, can help some students read with greater automaticity. You can also encourage the student to create their own such cards.

- Appendix D lists more than 75 multisensory practice ideas that, while focused on building spelling skills, also increase automaticity in word recognition, which increases fluency.

A resource for supported, repeated reading is the RAZ Plus® program we use for many students at Wings to Soar, which provides structured, repeated reading for different purposes including reading along with audio that models fluent reading (at an appropriate pace for the level), and reading independently and then recording themselves reading the passage aloud.

Vocabulary

As previously mentioned, dyslexics do not typically read as much as others, and this can lead to diminished vocabulary. One of the keys to building a strong vocabulary is to provide plenty of opportunity for students to listen to text at their level. In other words, read out loud to them. Most children enjoy being read to even if they're proficient readers themselves. It provides great family bonding time. You can also provide other means of access to ear-reading text through audio books or computer-read text. This builds both vocabulary and background knowledge. Working on phonics and fluency helps build eye-reading skills and should be practiced separately, but concurrently with building vocabulary and comprehension by tapping stronger ear-reading skills.

Most students benefit from targeted vocabulary work. Learning how to use vocabulary strategies to unlock new words opens up many more words. Recognizing word parts from previous studies and independently applying them to new vocabulary words is very empowering. I had one student share with me her excitement over how many words she was able to read during her ACT exam. She was in 10th grade, but her work in Wordly Wise 3000® was at levels four to six. Because of the strategies taught in that program, she felt confident about her work on a college entrance exam!

Resources and Strategies for Building Vocabulary

At Wings to Soar Online Academy we use several programs to explicitly build vocabulary:

- The online version of Wordly Wise 3000 focuses on building deep vocabulary connections, provides audio support, includes passages for building comprehension, and provides immediate feedback on answers. (Our free Just-Right Level™ Assessment includes a Wordly Wise 3000 placement assessment.)

- Word Build® addresses word-part-based vocabulary such as prefixes, suffixes, and roots. This is a natural extension of instruction for older students who have solid foundations in phonics. This type of vocabulary-building work is sometimes referred to as *structural analysis.*

- Lexia®, Reading Plus, and Moby Max are other online programs we use that have vocabulary-building sections. For non-struggling students these may be enough. For dyslexia and other challenges, these programs can supplement more intensive work in more targeted programs.

Other strategies to help build vocabulary include:

- Encourage the student to use new vocabulary words in daily conversation and in their writing.

- Discuss any multiple meanings of a word that are relevant to the student.

- When a student uses a word for which the context does not make its meaning clear, ask, "Do you mean _____ or _____ or something else?"

- Encourage use of a thesaurus while writing to add to the vocabulary. Using a thesaurus online is preferable to a printed one because it's easier to find the word you're looking for. Visual Thesaurus and www.thesaurus.com are good options.

- Make index cards with words on one side and their definitions on the other side. Review these throughout the day and use them to play games.

- Games to play to expand vocabulary:
  - Rummy Roots™ vocabulary-building games teach Latin and Greek word roots borrowed by the English language.
  - A fun, free resource for vocabulary building is www.freerice.com.
  - Play various matching games using synonyms and antonyms to build vocabulary, such as Concentration, Old Maid, and Go Fish.
  - Use any generic board game and move one space for each synonym or antonym a player can give for the vocabulary word-card that is drawn.

Comprehension

The ultimate goal of reading, of course, is comprehension. All the other skills addressed in this chapter are building blocks for comprehension.

Many dyslexics are very good at comprehension because of the way their brains are wired for reasoning, telling stories, making connections, and seeing an entire scene at once. The challenge lies in the skills leading up to comprehension: recognizing and distinguishing individual words, letters, and sounds. It's important to help dyslexics connect with prior knowledge so they can actively draw on that knowledge to gain meaning. It's very common for dyslexics to comprehend at a much higher level than that at which they can read aloud.

Reading for comprehension is a separate skill from reading out loud. Often students are asked to prove they can "actually read" a given text by reading a text out loud. For a dyslexic student this proves their inability to sound out words rather than their ability to comprehend, reinforcing their weakness and inadequacy. A better technique is to have the student read silently to themselves, then have them explain what they read in their own words, and use follow-up questions about specific knowledge. Requiring them to read aloud reinforces their weakness and inadequacy, while allowing them to demonstrate their comprehension builds confidence that they actually are readers who can get meaning from what they read. They should practice sounding out words at a different time.

Dyslexics who also have an underlying language-based learning disability may need the help of a speech and language therapist who is experienced in building the receptive and expressive language skills needed for comprehension. If the student has difficulty with comprehension, whether they are listening or reading themselves, it is a good indication that this angle of intervention should be explored through a comprehensive speech and language evaluation.

The following are simple strategies that build comprehension:

- The Davis Picture-at-Punctuation strategy encourages students to use their strong picture-thinking skills to create a picture in their mind each time they reach a punctuation mark. This is to ensure that they understand what's been read. As they become proficient at the phrase and sentence levels, it can be extended to the paragraph, page, and chapter levels.[7]

- To build context-based problem-solving skills, encourage the student to silently read quickly for context and overall meaning without stopping to figure out every word. This is not the time for working on decoding skills. This type of practice boosts stamina and interest in reading.

- Asking questions is likely the best way to support the growth of comprehension. The "5 Ws" (who, what, when, where, and why), plus "how," are a great start in constructing questions. Here are some sample questions:

  o Who are the main characters? What are they like?

  o What is happening in the story?

  o What seems to be the problem?

  o What might happen next? How did the student come to that conclusion?

  o When does the story take place? How is that important to the story?

  o How much time is passing?

  o Where is the story set? How does the setting of the story impact the telling of the story?

  o Why is a character acting a certain way? How did the student come to that conclusion?

Resources for Building Comprehension

Audio-supported text is an effective aid for many dyslexics in stretching their comprehension skills beyond what they can read independently. Wings to Soar uses the audio-supported online library RAZ-Plus, and many of our academic courses have audio support built in. We also recommend Learning Ally™ and Bookshare®.

It is important to work on comprehension skills for understanding both literature and informational text. Programs Wings to Soar uses that work directly on reading comprehension are MindPlay, Reading Plus, Headsprout Reading Comprehension, Lexia, and Moby Max. We make recommendations about which combination will best help each student based on assessment of their individual needs.

Students should master all five areas of reading: phonological and phonemic awareness, phonics, fluency, vocabulary, and comprehension. Weak skills in any area hamper full development of all the skills needed for reading. These skills build on one another, and students benefit from targeted practice to master earlier skills so they can truly excel in all skills. By doing so they can become independent, confident readers, even if they are best at ear-reading.

Chapter 5

Rethinking Learning – Spelling

Many dyslexic students who have gotten past (or never had) reading struggles still have great difficulty with spelling. While tools such as spell check and predictive text are incredibly helpful, some focused work on the most frequently used words and patterns can have a large payoff.

When I started using my training in Orton-Gillingham, I realized that some spelling patterns repeat with amazing frequency, while I had trouble coming up with more than a few words for other patterns. I employed my computer-programmer husband to write a custom program for analyzing the entire dictionary for any spelling pattern. I wanted to make sure I was teaching my students patterns that were truly useful. Over 14 years I researched to identify which patterns, and which words within those patterns, are the most used. I manually sorted the spelling patterns into their different sounds so I would confidently know how many words are in each of these patterns, or clusters.

Dyslexics don't tend to be incidental learners; that is, they do not automatically pick up patterns and rules. One of Dr. Orton's findings is that dyslexics need direct, systematic instruction that makes the rules and patterns explicit. They need to be taught the patterns as well as the rules and generalizations that go with them. The amount of phonics in most spelling curricula is not enough for dyslexics. It also goes way too fast for them.

Dyslexic students have trouble learning such rules, so why bother with the ones that are so infrequently relevant? If you still have doubts, take a look at the below frequencies-of-use in written English:

Top 300 words   65%
Top 1,000 words   90%
Top 2,000 words   95%
Top 3,000 words   97%

It makes sense to focus time and effort on high-frequency patterns and words. Any other pattern or word can be taught as it becomes personally useful to the student.

The Wings to Soar Spelling Foundations program is the direct result of my extensive research. And I have included the highest-frequency words in these phonetic patterns in appendix E.

For learning to spell, I classify words into three categories:
● Phonetically regular words with high-frequency patterns that are worth learning
● "Outlaw words" – small groups of words that "break the rules together"
● True "rule-breakers" that just need to be memorized

For phonetically regular words, repetitions of words within a family of related words reinforces connections between the words. Learning "outlaw words" as clusters reinforces their connections to each other. There are few enough of them in each cluster that Wings to Soar Spelling Foundations provides sentences for some of the "outlaw families" using them all. The sentences are picturable even if individual words are not. Once the student knows the words in an outlaw family they know not to guess that spelling for words not in that family. For rule-breakers I recommend using the multisensory strategies and Daily Basic 5 practice over the course of two or three weeks so the student can get the repetitions needed to add the word to their long-term memory. I provide these multisensory practice ideas in appendix D.

The more we use a neural pathway, the more efficient it becomes. This is why repetition is so important. Research has shown that it takes 60 to 75 repetitions of a word spelled correctly to get the word into long-term memory.[1] How many repetitions are there in a typical spelling lesson – five, or maybe ten? Maybe the parent quizzes the student another five or ten times. Perhaps the student writes the word ten times. That is only 30 repetitions, possibly enough to pass the test on Friday, but not enough to get it into long-term memory. Natural spellers get most of these repetitions through just reading the words. This kind of practice is more than adequate for them, but is not enough for dyslexics.

The "see it, say it, write it" principle that Orton-Gillingham uses provides important multisensory feedback to the brain. That is essential for helping dyslexics internalize the phonetic patterns for spelling mastery. However, I found that many students need even more multisensory stimulation to keep them engaged enough to learn. I have gathered more than 75 different multisensory practice ideas to further connect with visual, tactile, and kinesthetic learners. My Daily Basic 5 practice recommendations and this list of multisensory strategies can be found in appendix D.

Many phonics programs have the student memorize all the possible sounds for a spelling pattern. But for many spellings there are one to four patterns that are common; the other patterns often only apply to a small number of words. I prefer to have students learn the words containing these less common patterns as clusters of outlaw words that break the rules together.

A good example of this is the *ou* spelling pattern. The *ou* vowel combination makes six different sounds in English (pronounce the words *sound*, *rough*, *four*, *group*, *could*, and *soul*);

however, only the /ou/ sound is common (as in *round*, *out*, *foul*, etc.). It is, in fact, a very common vowel-team pattern. Teach the rule that **ou** is never used at the end of a syllable, and that if the /ow/ sound comes at the end of a word, to use the **ow** pattern. Learning both in tandem is more useful than either by itself. The **ow** spelling for /ow/ is not used unless it's at the end of a syllable or followed by *n* or *l*.

The rest of the sounds that **ou** can make are very uncommon. For example, I want students to learn *enough*, *rough*, and *tough* together because these three words (and their variants, such as *roughly* and *tougher*) are the only ones that use that pattern. A sample memory-aid sentence is "I am tough enough to do rough work." Another outlaw family with only three words is *could*, *would*, and *should*. Here's a sample sentence for that group: "I would go if I could, but I should stay home." Teach them together. If the student learns these two clusters of outlaw words, each of the words in each cluster becomes a reminder of the other words in the pattern. Do students need to worry about using **ou** for other words, or yet another pattern, making our language more complex than it needs to be?

I have found it's best to teach similar sounds separately. This is essential for many dyslexics due to their weakness with fine details. For example, many programs teach the short vowels in alphabetical order. For those with phonological-processing issues, this is one of the worst possible orders to learn. Many individuals who struggle with reading and spelling have great difficulty distinguishing between the sounds of the short *e* and short *i*. When these two similar sounds are taught in alphabetical order, it amplifies the confusion because the student can't hear the difference.

I have also discovered that it's best to separate the teaching of similar visual spelling patterns. Some programs unnecessarily confuse students by teaching all of the vowel teams that start with *o* in succession. For example, it can be useful to teach **ou** as the spelling at the beginning and in the middle of syllables and **ow** as the spelling at the end of syllables (or when followed by *n* or *l*) at the same time. It's wise to give the brain time to solidify those patterns with extensive practice before introducing the **oi** and **oy** pairs, for example, which have a similar rule (**oy** occurs only at the end of syllables, just like **ow**).

I'm always looking for possible stumbling blocks for my struggling learners. I try to eliminate, or at least minimize, such blocks. I have taken all of these things into account when writing my Wings to Soar Spelling Foundations program.

At Wings to Soar some students have found that the phonetic-skills practices in MindPlay, Lexia, Nessy, and Reading Horizons are adequate in addressing their spelling challenges. Many also benefit from the focused work in Wings to Soar Spelling Foundations.

Wings to Soar Spelling Options

For the older student with kindergarten through second-grade-level phonetic-reading skills, but who has spelling gaps, I encourage you to request Wings to Soar's free Spelling Dictation Placement Sentences, which incorporates 756 words that make up 71 percent of written English. If the student's profile of needs suggests these are appropriate, you'll receive them when you request your free Just-Right Level Assessments at www.JustRightLevel.com. The Spelling Dictation Placement Sentences are meant for parents to use at home to assess which words your child needs to work on. I have found that many older, struggling spellers have difficulty with at least a quarter to as many as two-thirds of these high-frequency words. These are words we typically expect to be learned in first or second grade.

Whether or not you choose to work with our Wings to Soar Spelling Foundations or Customized Remedial Spelling, I encourage you to work on the words you identify in this assessment. These are more important than any random words in anyone's spelling program. Supplement these with the student's personal spelling demons – the words they spell incorrectly when they write. This is important because if repetition causes the wrong neural pathways to form, it can take 600 to 2,000 correct repetitions to rewire the brain! The more a wrong spelling has been reinforced, the more repetitions are required to accomplish the rewiring. Catching and correcting errors as early as possible minimizes such setbacks.

It's best to correct spelling before a mistake lodges in long-term memory. If misspelling recurs in later writing after a student has worked through the first round of the Daily Basic 5 practice, immediately re-add the word to their current spelling list. Practice again for another week or two of Daily Basic 5 practice. Then move it to weekly review for a month. You might need to do this many times if the word was originally learned incorrectly. Do not try for 600 repetitions during one round of learning; just come back as often as misuse suggests rewiring is still a work in process.

My Wings to Soar Spelling Foundations program focuses on the top 3,000 words in written English, making up 97 percent of the words we write. If 3,000 words can make up 97 percent of our language, why bother with the thousands of additional words that make up the other 3 percent until the student has use for them?

Focus on only the additional words that are truly useful to the student in writing about their areas of interest. This is especially true for the dyslexic, who is going to excel at other real-world skills. Then add their "personal passion" words. For a student interested in football, words like *quarterback, field, receiver,* and *touchdown* are important words to master. For a student interested in ballet, *tutu, relevé, choreographer,* and *ballet* are important to add to their personal repertoire. I encourage you to allow your student to use topics of personal interest for their writing assignments unless they are doing a paper for an academic topic. If they are not likely to use a particular word in the future, make a vocabulary card for reference and don't waste their emotional energy memorizing its spelling.

Consistently spaced repetition and review helps the brain build the neural pathways for long-term retention. "Use it or lose it" is a core principle in learning. Encourage usage in real life, not just on worksheets. Challenge students to use their new spelling and/or vocabulary words in their writing and in daily conversation.

Chapter 6

Rethinking Learning – Writing

Writing is made up of many small skills that together create "chunks" of skill sets. Like an orchestra, these skill sets must work together in concert to create a piece of work that feels harmonious, unified, and whole. If any section of the orchestra (or single instrument) is out of tune or off beat, the whole performance suffers. In the same way, any unmastered skill in writing causes the entire process to suffer. As beautiful, creative, spontaneous, or imaginative as music and writing can be, there is a skill-based side that requires practice and dedication. In music, if a trumpet player cannot control their breath well, the sound that comes out is squeaky and shrill. A drummer must practice keeping an even tempo or they will mislead an entire band. Writing is the same way. Any skill that is not mastered is like that shrill note, that skip in the rhythm, or simply that lack of spark that puts the audience to sleep.

Writing is hard, and struggling students need support as they practice each individual skill and slowly put them all together. With support they will discover the feeling of having created a masterpiece, with each skill playing with the rest and no one skill more noticeable than the other. All is in harmony and the work flows out from the skills in a beautiful symphony.

What Is Good Writing? The 6+1Traits® of Writing

In the 1980s a model called "The Six Traits of Writing" was developed by a large group of teachers nationwide. The goals of this writing model were to:

- Create a list of common characteristics that appear in "good writing"

- Create a way to teach and evaluate the complex process of writing

- Create a shared vocabulary about writing

- Create and foster feedback between writers and teachers that celebrates the ever-developing process of writing, not just the products of writing

This model is widely adopted in US schools, and anyone working with developing writers should have an understanding of it. This source is suggested for further reading: www.educationnorthwest. org/traits/about-61-trait-writing.

According to this model there are six traits that appear in all good writing. They are:

- **Ideas:** the main message

- **Organization:** the internal structure of the piece

- **Word Choice:** the vocabulary a writer chooses to convey meaning

- **Sentence Fluency:** the rhythm and flow of the language

- **Voice:** the personal tone and flavor of the author's message

- **Conventions:** the mechanical correctness – punctuation, capitalization, spelling, usage, and grammar[1]

And Education Northwest's writing model adds one more:

- **Presentation (the "+ 1" Trait):** how the writing actually looks and/or sounds. Formatting can vary depending on the media being used for presentation.[2]

The Writing Process

Breaking writing down into a step-by-step process makes it manageable. Each stage in the writing process takes the writer another step from idea to polished piece. This is the same process that professional writers use. No professional writer expects the first draft to be great. They know that many rounds of revising and editing help them turn their initial start into the final form. According to *Write Source*, there are five stages to the writing process:

- Prewriting
  - Brainstorm using mind maps, lists, etc.
  - Select your topic: What is the subject of my writing?
  - Determine your audience: Who will read the writing? What are their needs, biases, and prior knowledge?
  - Determine your purpose: Why am I writing? What is my goal?
  - Select your writing type: What type of writing is appropriate for this piece?
    - Descriptive: a detailed picture of a person, place, thing, or event
    - Narrative: relates an event, experience, or story
    - Persuasive: persuades the reader to agree with the writer about something
    - Expository: explains by presenting steps, causes, or kinds of something
  - Understand the list of criteria against which you will measure your output.
  - Gather information.
    - What do I know? What don't I know?
    - Read and find out more about the topic and the audience.
    - Take notes (note the sources in your notes so you can provide proper citations).
  - Organize your thoughts into an overall plan.
- Drafting
  - Use the prewriting plan as a guide, but add and adapt as appropriate as you write.
  - Concentrate on getting the ideas down on paper when writing the first draft. Don't try to make it perfect. That comes later.

o Use dictation or speech-to-text if you wish help in getting your thoughts onto the page. Google Documents has a free tool called Voice Typing that makes this easy.

o Explain the main message in a way that makes sense.

o Group the supporting details into a logical sequence.

o Find and insert supporting evidence, details, etc.

o Compose the introduction, body, and conclusion for each paragraph and for the piece as a whole.

o Cite sources as you draft (but you can format them in the editing stage).

- Revising

o If the rough draft was not created on a computer, it is well worth inputting the text in a word processing program such as Google Documents or Microsoft Word before beginning the multi-stage revision process. This will make revising much easier and more effective.

o Review each draft after setting it aside for a while so you can see it with fresh eyes.

o Work through the writing piece several times. Each time focus on one of the following traits of good writing:

- **Ideas:** Have you communicated the main message clearly? Effective writing has a clear message, purpose, and focus. Have you used plenty of specific ideas and details to support your main message?

- **Organization:** Does the writing follow a coherent plan? Is there a weaving together of ideas? Does the structure of the piece make sense? Do all the ideas in each paragraph support the main point of the paragraph? Is there a clear beginning, middle, and end to each paragraph and to the piece as a whole? Have you used strong transition words and phrases appropriate to the type of writing to connect ideas, such as "Next," "For this reason," "For example," and "On the other hand"?

- **Word Choice:** Are the words chosen the best words to convey meaning? Does your choice of words convey a formal or more personal and informal tone as appropriate to the piece? Are the nouns and verbs specific? Are the adjectives and adverbs clear and colorful? Does the word choice allow for clear yet concise writing? Is a word overused? If so, look for more powerful synonyms to vary the word choice. Make sure the words you choose are words your audience will understand.

- **Sentence Fluency:** Are the sentences different in length, sentence type, opening words, and complexity, providing variety? Does the rhythm and flow of the language work for this piece? Do the sentences read smoothly and flow from one to the next? Listen as someone else reads your piece aloud. Do any of the sentences cause the reader to stumble or sound awkward?

- **Voice:** Are the tone and flavor appropriate to the piece and audience? Are they consistent? Have you demonstrated your unique viewpoints on the topic? Does your writing show your genuine interest in the topic? Do you come across as knowledgeable and confident about your topic? Do you appropriately share your honest feelings and thoughts about the topic?

  o Share working drafts for feedback. Does what you wrote communicate what you want to say to your intended audience?

- Editing
  o This is the stage for proofreading for the *conventions* of good writing: grammar, usage, pronoun reference, consistency in number and person, and mechanics (spelling, capitalization, punctuation, paragraphing, and proper formatting of citations).
  o Measure the final product against a given criteria or rubric.

- Publishing
  o Make sure the *presentation* of the final piece is neat and follows guidelines for margins, spacing, and indenting.
  o Share the finished writing with others.
  o Use appropriate modes (print, multimedia, etc.) for the audience and purpose.[3]

Consistent Practice

Good writing is the ultimate goal for our students. Developing writing fluency takes the student from merely manipulating words and phrases to communicating and emotionally connecting with another person through the written word. Automaticity in applying the skills needed for fluent writing is developed through regular, daily practice. Like any learning process, learning writing needs an active, consistent *spiral sequence* to create automaticity and reliability, whereby topics are introduced, practiced, and then built upon further.

Each writing trait needs to be practiced in isolation, in chunks, and within the writing process, no matter the learning level of the writer. Each trait can be difficult for those who are challenged by higher-order thinking skills, processing skills, etc. So how do teachers teach this and students practice this?

Below is a suggested breakdown of how to structure writing sessions using the traditional six traits of writing. Students, regardless of ability, must write daily to become skilled writers.

- Six traits in isolation
  - Workbook or online application drills: grammar, parts of speech, punctuation, vocabulary, spelling, prefixes/suffixes, synonyms/antonyms, sentence construction
    - Vocabulary: 10 to 20 minutes daily
    - Spelling: 10 minutes daily
    - Grammar, usage, mechanics: 10 minutes daily
  - Immediate feedback from parent or computer program
- Six traits in chunks
  - Identifying and applying elements of paragraph writing (including grammar)
  - Crafting introductions, body paragraphs, and extended paragraphs
  - Peer/partner revision and editing

- o The Writing Skills series by Diana Hanbury King from Educators Publishing Service is great for this kind of practice.
  - o 10 to 20 minutes two or three times per week until these traits are mastered
- Six traits in action
  - o The student should spend time journaling or free writing on topics of their own choosing. The goal is to increase fluidity in getting their thoughts on paper.
  - o This type of writing should not be critiqued. Revision, editing, and publishing are not appropriate for this session.
  - o 10 to 20 minutes two or three times per week
- Six traits in a written piece
  - o The student should take one piece of writing through the full writing process (as described above) over the course of a week or two.
  - o Paragraph and/or essay formats
  - o Project management taught as they work on the longer-term project
  - o Constant review of the writing rubric throughout the process
  - o 20 to 30 minutes daily

In our writing courses at Wings to Soar Online Academy we build all of these elements into the day-to-day assignments for our students using the appropriate online programs, workbooks, and writing handbooks for each student's level.

The following is a chart of different types of writing Wings to Soar students do throughout the school year to apply the six traits of writing to written pieces. Each year they write at least three types from each section (both short and long). We link these to the topics they are studying in social studies, so the curriculum drives the type of writing they do. Consider how these might link to your curriculum.

Argumentative/ Persuasive	Informative/Explanatory	Narrative/Descriptive
Present a claim or point of view logically, and with strong evidence.	Present new information and/or help a reader understand a topic.	Present unfolding stories and reflections with vibrant descriptions.
• Compare/contrast	• How-to (process)	• Short story
• Cause-and-effect	• Summary, paraphrase	• Novel
• Problem/solution	• Expository	• Biography, autobiography
• Argumentation: researched statement of claim	• Research	• Folklore (legend, myth, folktale, fable)
	• Technical writing	• Personal narrative, other forms of self-expression (poetry, lyrics, plays, etc.)

Obstacle for Writers: Taking Risks

For all writers the process is at some point daunting. When we don't know what to do next, writing becomes challenging and feels beyond what we can do. We call this "writer's block," but a more accurate name would be "writer's torture"!

Students need to be taught that it is okay, and even necessary, to take small risks in writing that require them to step out of their comfort zone. This needs to be done carefully, consistently, and in a way that promotes a successful experience. If a student can learn to take writing risks no matter what the challenge, they will become a competent writer. Writing well is like performing well: it will happen if you take the time to work on fundamentals as well as application.

To apply skills successfully, developing writers are encouraged to take risks that are hard for their current learning level. The only reason writing seems difficult or impossible for many learning-challenged kids is that no adult has yet broken down learning the skills into manageable steps at just the right level of challenge for them in each skill strand. There is no reason a dyslexic student can't learn to become a good writer if you scaffold the process and provide supports as needed.

Failure to build component skills prior to combining them into a finished product yields unsuccessful results. For example, neither teacher nor student should expect a first draft to be the final product. Such failures precondition the student to avoid risks. Wading into the writing process one step at a time is much safer than trying to dive in all at once. The student learns to think, "Yes, there is a little risk, but I can step back and take a step in a different direction (revise) when I need to. I might stub my toe, but I won't break my neck. It will take longer, but I will eventually reach my goal of effective communication safely."

Writing at Wings to Soar: Feedback; Benchmarks; Common Vocabulary; Chunking, Sequencing, and Pacing; Scaffolding

The six-traits model helps everyone at Wings to Soar see the big picture of what good writing looks like. It also provides the framework for progress and skill development.

Feedback

All writers need feedback from a variety of people to know whether their efforts are headed in the right direction. While the writer can internally comment on the piece, it takes another's eye to help the writer see what the reader sees. To be effective, feedback must come through many modes of communication. Banish the red pen! Replace it with:

- Asking open-ended questions (see "Essential Questions" in appendix C)
- Reading a work in progress out loud

- Recording reading the work in progress and listening to how it sounds
- Color-coding sections that show one or more of the six traits
- Literally cutting apart a printed copy of the writing into sections and reordering the parts on a tabletop, then reading the new arrangement out loud
  - Substitute words to create clearer sentences.
  - Rearrange, add, or delete sentences for better paragraphs.
  - Rearrange paragraphs for better organization.
- Using "copy" and "paste" on a computer to do the same thing is also effective.
- If a particular section is well written, but not appropriate for the current piece, it's helpful to copy it to a "parking lot" document to save it for possible future use. (See more about using parking lots in appendix C.) This makes cutting something that the student has worked hard on more palatable.

Benchmarks

Our rating scales include descriptions with terms that both teachers and students understand to use as benchmarks. Benchmarks are usually presented in a grid format and called a rubric. If you google "six traits writing rubrics" in your browser, you will quickly find dozens of well-crafted rubrics made by teachers that contain:

- A rating system
  - Usually from 1 (lowest) to 5 or 6 (highest)
  - A corresponding description of the rating
    - 1 = beginning, needs work, novice, or other generalization that implies inexperience, to
    - 5 or 6 = exemplary, fluent, or other generalization that implies complete mastery with flair
- A brief description of each of the six traits
- A description of what the trait looks like at that particular rating using words that have a shared meaning for students and teachers

Where Are My Student's Writing Skills Right Now?

Below is the rubric we use to assess which level of our writing program would be the best fit for an incoming student. Find the general description(s) that fit(s) your student right now.

	Minimal	Basic	Developing	Proficient	Advanced
Ideas	Idea fragments	Stream-of-consciousness, little development	Complete thoughts, basic idea development	Complete thoughts, examples, proof; may need to refine	Well-developed, detailed, sound logic/sequence, drives to a successful conclusion
Organization	Fragmented	Ideas clustered, attempt at format	Expanded paragraphs used	Consistent, longer writing shows understanding of essay format	Strong, accurate, shows flair
Word Choice	Very limited	Limited to personal vocabulary	Personal vocabulary, content words, might try advanced vocabulary if directed	Consistent, advanced vocabulary seen	Precise, consistent advanced vocabulary, matches audience, style
Sentence Fluency	Very limited, no format, words and phrases	Sentence fragments, run-ons, little variety in those that are complete	Simple sentences; some variety in sentence types, including compound and complex sentences	Variety of sentence types keeps reader interested	Strategic use of varied sentences, shows flair and style
Voice/Style	Insufficient sample to evaluate	Undeveloped	Attempt to connect with audience; point of view/voice seen	Knows purpose and audience, interesting	Purpose and audience clear; engaging, thought provoking, insightful, surprising, unique
Conventions	Fragmented, missing	Sporadic, not consistent	Fundamental, some errors	Consistent, few/no errors, typical	Strong, creative, few/no errors

What Does "Proficient Writing" Look Like?

We know that chronological ages and ability levels differ, and place students accordingly. Not sure of your child's current level? Find the general description(s) that fit(s) below. This chart shows what the proficient column would look like at each of these skill levels for three major categories of writing.

Argumentative/ Persuasive	Informative/Explanatory	Narrative/Descriptive
Present a claim or point of view logically, and with strong evidence.	Present new information and/or help a reader understand a topic.	Present unfolding stories and reflections with vibrant descriptions.
Benchmark: "Proficient looks like…"	**Benchmark:** "Proficient looks like…"	**Benchmark:** "Proficient looks like…"
☐ **Elementary Level:** Student clearly states their opinion and reasons with examples for proof in logical, well-formed, expanded paragraphs. ☐ **MS Level:** Student articulates both sides of an issue, then logically explains their position supported with evidence. ☐ **HS Level:** Student defends concise, logically sound statements of claims with researched, cited evidence. Counterclaims and rebuttals are anticipated and addressed.	☐ **Elementary Level:** In expanded paragraphs student presents reasoned, researched answers to questions like "How are stories from other places and times about me?"[4] ☐ **MS Level:** Student logically, accurately explains concepts and events using examples to highlight important points for a specific purpose. ☐ **HS Level:** After identifying an audience and developing a research plan, student presents concepts and ideas for the purpose of uncovering themes, trends, and unique insights.	☐ **Elementary/MS Level:** Narrative shows a clear sequence of events (or development of ideas) with rich detail. Individual creativity is celebrated by sharing narrative work with other students for constructive feedback. A variety of samples allows for practice of various narrative types. ☐ **HS Level:** Narratives show variation; creative strengths (and risk-taking); smoothness; clarity of ideas; creative, logical organization; use of drama; and reflect life change.[5]

Common (Shared) Vocabulary

Our rubrics describe what the student and the teacher see (or want to see) in the work. Our students should have a good understanding of the writing rubric before they begin a writing assignment so they know what is expected of them. This supports our belief that a student must take charge of the quality and completeness of their work.

A shared vocabulary of observable characteristics is key to giving and receiving feedback. At Wings to Soar we evaluate all writing using the vocabulary in our rubrics. Students and teachers use this vocabulary when giving and receiving feedback. When communicating with parents we use this same vocabulary so everyone on the team is speaking the same language.

Chunking, Sequencing, and Pacing

"Chunking" links skills (or skill sets) together in "chunks" to create a desirable result. The quality of the final product grows as each chunk is mastered. In the end, quality is ensured because the chunks have been evaluated and refined along the way. The size, sequence (what is presented and when), and pacing (amount of time spent) of the chunks depend on the overall skill level and the learning needs of the student.

Scaffolding

Steel scaffolds are used when a construction project is being built or repaired. They provide a safe platform for the workers. As the building is completed, they are removed. Wings to Soar created a series of writing *scaffolds* that help bridge the gaps between brainstorming, outlining, working drafts, and the final product. They work in the same way as physical scaffolds, providing structure and "safety" as a draft is being constructed, and are removed once the writing is strong enough to stand on its own. This helps with organization, detail, sequence, development of ideas, and focus. The student copies and pastes the scaffold into their document. After they have used the supports provided, they delete the scaffold before turning in their assignment.

Below is an example of a persuasive-essay scaffold we created and use at Wings to Soar. We teach what the terms in the scaffolds mean and use scaffolds like this for all writing with students.

Persuasive Essay Scaffold

Copy and paste this into your writing. When you have a good version that is in your own words, erase the scaffold and leave your writing.

Introductory Paragraph

===========

A "hook" (a quote, provocative statement, unusual fact or statistic, engaging question, etc.):

Thesis (a claim that is both arguable and defensible):

Preview of points (1 to 3) that support your claim:

Springboard or transition statement (to flow into the body):

Body (Evidence 1)

=============

Transition (to flow into the defense). Restate point #1:

Evidence:

Prove its credibility:

Three details to show how this evidence proves the claim:

Transition – introduce a counterclaim for point #1:

Counterclaim (rebuttal evidence):

Evidence:

Prove its credibility:

Overcome the counterclaim by showing where the evidence fails to prove it:

Body (Evidence 2)

==============

SAME

Body (Evidence 3)

=============

SAME

Concluding paragraph

================

Summation transition ("In conclusion" or some other concluding phrase):

Restatement of thesis (new words, stated in a way that shows successful proof):

Review of three pieces of evidence (hit the highlights of the evidence and show how it overcomes the counterclaim):

Clincher – leave us with a provocative thought that makes us "go away" from your paper wanting to learn more about it. Or call us to act further on this idea, or challenge us.

As we've seen, the writing process is complex. Start at the student's current level. Practice doable skill chunks. Provide specific feedback at each step. This will gradually increase their skills toward proficiency. When taken one step at a time, it does not have to be overwhelming.

Chapter 7

Revisioning Dyslexia Intervention

Our mission at Wings to Soar Online Academy is to break the chains of failure, inadequacy, and shame so often associated with dyslexia and other outside-the-box learning needs. We address the whole person, building the skills and confidence to thrive and succeed in school and life, not just survive. We do this by creating a Path to Success Personalized Learning Plan for each student. We start with free Just-Right Level Assessments, which can be requested at www.JustRightLevel.com, to identify each student's specific skill gaps.

Based on the findings from the Just-Right Level Assessments and insights from the parent during a complimentary Path to Success Curriculum Consultation, our intervention specialist recommends a Path to Success Personalized Learning Plan from more than 25 different online programs offered through Wings to Soar. Not only do we offer years of experience, training, and expertise, but our free trial allows us to hone in on just the right combination of programs for each student with a lot less hassle and much quicker results than parents having to figure it out themselves. Our progress monitoring increases the odds that students will make effective use of the programs. This means parents are no longer alone in monitoring their child's education. They have a partner. They have information about their child's performance to guide the daily check-in and check-out they should have with their child. Students have an additional outside source for accountability.

We begin at the student's actual functional level in each skill area, backing up from where they've been working if necessary. Far more useful than a general "reading level," we break it down to the foundational skills of phonemic awareness, phonics, fluency, vocabulary, and comprehension. The assessments also address spelling, grammar, usage, and mechanics, and provide a snapshot of the student's functional writing level. We do the same for math, with gaps identified in each skill strand. By working at their Just-Right Level in each skill area, the student is challenged, but at a level at which they can achieve confident and independent success.

We bump up the overall time and intensity with short practice sessions in a few different programs. This strategy allows for needed repetition and practice so the student's brain can build neural pathways for automaticity of the skills. This allows their brain adequate time to assimilate the learning, which does not occur when a similar amount of practice time is devoted to a single program, even if the program itself is of high quality. It also minimizes student resistance and maximizes engagement with the programs. Using several programs provides variety and keeps any one program from becoming boring.

The programs we use are diagnostic and prescriptive, meaning they are built to identify what the student knows and doesn't know, while constantly adjusting the learning path based on the student's responses. If the student cannot grasp a concept in one program, more than likely presenting it in a different way in another program will help them get it. Once the student has mastered the skill, each program automatically moves on without unnecessary repetition of already-learned skills. The power of the quality, adaptive, computer-based programs we've chosen is that quite often a click of the mouse literally determines what instruction the student will receive next. The program mix we use includes more programs than any one student will use, and is constantly being updated as we find programs that do an even better job.

Most dyslexics need one to three years of an Orton-Gillingham phonics-based approach. Wings to Soar uses a custom combination of online programs that support core Orton-Gillingham principles. We get faster results with far less resistance and lower cost than I ever achieved doing one-to-one Orton-Gillingham tutoring. While each of these programs is useful individually, the way we recommend using them together achieves more powerful results.

In addition to a solid phonics foundation, many students also need focused instruction and practice to strengthen visual tracking, efficiency, stamina, fluency, comprehension, and vocabulary. Practice reading audio-supported material on a wide variety of subjects builds background knowledge, vocabulary, and interest in reading. One program we offer provides this at gradually increasing levels of difficulty, with each word highlighted as it is read aloud to support visual recognition of words. We also offer programs that provide supplementary instruction and specific practice in comprehension skills, vocabulary development, and language skills such as grammar, usage, and mechanics.

While we work on building foundational reading skills, students can begin to explore writing on an informal basis, largely with the parent acting as scribe so the student can get used to the idea of being a writer. Once students have at least a solid third-grade reading level, we move them into our more structured writing curriculum with instruction and feedback from our writing coach. Powerful scaffolds we've developed support students in learning how to write paragraphs, then expanded paragraphs, and finally essays in a variety of genres. Once students are able to write paragraphs we add a computer program with powerful artificial-intelligence feedback and built-in skill instruction, as well as regular one-to-one sessions with our writing coach.

As a student begins to work in their Path to Success Personalized Learning Plan, they are encouraged to go as slowly as they need to, but as quickly as they are ready to. Targeted reteaching is built into many of the programs as needed. The goal is mastery, not mere coverage of the curriculum. As the student uses their intervention plan, we monitor their progress and make adjustments if necessary. Students do not progress at the same rate in all areas, so the balance of the mix might need adjusting from time to time to get the maximum benefit. After all, we are teaching a child, not a curriculum. The quality online curricula we choose are merely tools.

Wings to Soar is dedicated to student achievement in learning. We want to see students succeed. However "we" is not only our staff. It includes the parent(s) as well. Our staff provides expertise in curricula, learning challenges, and strategies. Parents know their children. They have struggled with them and have seen what works and what doesn't. They experience their children at their best and their worst, their strengths and their challenges. We are co-teachers of these children. For example, a parent can choose to reward a student with extra time in a program they love as motivation to complete something they resist. Or a student's health or family circumstances might necessitate modifications in a group class assignment for a particular student at a particular time. Although all assignments are already customized to the student's needs, external circumstances can't always be predicted. Wings to Soar works with parents to adjust accordingly. We do not work only with the child; we work within the framework of the child's entire life, including family life.

To do this effectively we need to build a solid, working relationship with the parent, who is co-teacher, through regular communication. Monitored progress reports can tell you only so much. Parents need to be on the front lines every day, observing how their child interacts with the programs. Wings to Soar greatly values parent feedback so that we can help each family even more expertly with their child's learning needs. Parents need to ensure that the changes suggested by the progress reports are implemented. Is the required time being put in? Are assignments completed? If things continue being done in the same way as before, one can't expect improved results.

Students respond better when there are multiple sources of accountability supporting each other. Teachers can't be effective when parents do not support them. Parents must enforce implementation of suggestions the teacher makes for improvement, or communicate why they are impractical so that the teacher can make other suggestions.

The teacher is responsible for teaching, making and correcting assignments, and providing feedback on progress or the lack thereof. Parents are ultimately responsible for seeing that the student does the work. They must also communicate with the teacher when they perceive a need for modifications.

Parent and student interactions with our teachers take our whole-person, child-centered (in the context of the family) approach to a whole new level. Through one-to-one and small-group webcam interaction, our teachers help dyslexics and other outside-the-box learners gain the confidence and skills they need to succeed in school and in life.

For families that choose to homeschool, we offer science and social studies courses at the middle school and high school levels. We use quality online curricula that include full audio support for text, while other content is presented through images, video, and virtual labs. Wings to Soar emphasizes comprehension, not spitting back facts, at all levels. Quizzes and tests are not emphasized, and are open-note. The student's understanding is demonstrated through weekly small-group webcam discussions that are considered far more important than tests.

At the middle school and high school levels, we weave social studies, literature, and composition together to create a series of classes that we call Integrated Liberal Studies. The reading and writing assignments do double-duty in more than one subject area; for example, a composition assignment builds on a history lesson. At the high school level, our rich, four-year Integrated Liberal Studies sequence uses history as the organizing spine and weaves in art and music appreciation, government, economics, archeology, anthropology, philosophy and religion, literature, and composition. Students make deep connections with the subject matter and find that diverse fields have relevance to each other. Students learn through a variety of approaches including reading (and/or listening), watching videos, small-group webcam discussions, writing about what they're learning, virtual field trips, debates, and role-playing. Using a variety of methods for taking in content taps in to the dyslexic strengths of contextual learning and interaction. Integrated Liberal Studies embraces diverse learning styles, making it ideal for many students, dyslexic or not, struggling or not.

Students receive a rich education that is usually only available to those with strong reading and writing skills. We are able to offer this experience by keeping their individual ability levels and challenges in mind and making accommodations as necessary. Assignments can be modified to fit the student's skill level. As stated before, Wings to Soar staff members have the expertise, but parents are co-teachers. As such, they have our permission to make any adjustment to any assignment that their child needs in order to be successful. Accommodations are standard and normal at Wings to Soar. We encourage accommodations such as speech-to-text, audio support, and parents as scribes for all students who would benefit from them.

A student's whole-person well-being is more important than any given assignment. While we have high expectations for our students, we understand that some days are more challenging than others. We provide a healthy balance of grace and accountability. If the student has a non-academic opportunity or need that temporarily outweighs a particular assignment being completed on time, our teachers work with the student to make sure that what is important receives the focus it deserves. We ask that parents communicate with us about why changes were necessary, though if a parent has a tendency to excuse their child from assignments or ignore progress reports too often we will call it to their attention and initiate a conversation to see how we can best work together. If the student is to make gains in overcoming their deficits, an adequate amount of work at an appropriate level is needed.

Wings to Soar Online Academy offers:

- quality curriculum that is customized to your child's needs
- an approach that centers around your child's whole-person well-being
- innovative accommodations and modifications

I invite you to get your child started with our free Just-Right Level Assessments today at www.JustRightLevel.com. Whether or not you choose to enroll your student in any of our programs, knowing at what level your child is actually functioning should guide your educational choices. No child is a grade-level package. Every child functions at different levels in different subject areas, and even in different strands of the subject. Backing up and filling in gaps completes a foundation for further learning. We ask you to ignore concerns about where your child "should" be functioning. Work intensively at the level at which they really are, and eventually they will get to where they should be.

Appendix A

Dyslexia Intervention Options

Getting Help in the Schools

Schools vary widely in how well they are able to provide remediation and support for dyslexic kids. If you suspect a learning problem and want to have your child evaluated by the school to see whether they might qualify for special education services, you have the right to request that evaluation (in writing). By law, schools must begin such an evaluation within a defined period of time, which in many states is 45 days. Many schools use a formal response-to-intervention (RTI) approach as a part of the process to see whether the student qualifies for special education services. It first has to be determined that the student is not making adequate gains in the presence of quality instruction, through research-based intervention, before identifying the student as having a learning disability.

If your child qualifies for special-education services after a series of assessments and meetings, a plan which in the US is called an Individualized Education Program (IEP) will be created outlining specific goals and services to help your child meet those goals.

Your knowledgeable requests for appropriate accommodations as outlined in appendix B can help your child get the support they need. The school, however, is under no obligation to provide any specific intervention or accommodation. It may not be able to afford to provide this sort of support through either financial or human resources.

Seeking Help Outside the School

In practice, a child usually needs to be two years behind to qualify for services. If you recognize the need before then, do not wait for the system to further handicap your child. Begin intervention immediately. This will likely need to be at your own expense.

Even when a child does qualify for special-education accommodations and services and the school is able to provide them, many parents find that they really need additional targeted remediation outside of school.

Far too often we've found that students in fifth and sixth grades and in middle school have to spend so much time on day-to-day homework just to keep their heads above water that little time and energy is left for remediation during the school year. For these students we recommend a summer intensive intervention program to make as many gains as possible during the summer. Such focused intervention is a much better use of their summer than "more of the same" summer school. Wings to Soar provides afterschool and summer intensive intervention to supplement the support provided (or not) in the public school.

During the school year the student should focus most of their energy on keeping up with current academic demands. But their brain needs to use their newly developing skills so they don't lose any gains they have made, so a less intensive maintenance program should be employed during the school year.

Most general tutoring centers, such as Sylvan, Huntington, Kumon, and others like them, don't provide the kind of focused, intensive intervention that gets at the core of learning challenges for a dyslexic. They are a better fit for a student who is just struggling a bit in school rather than for someone with a true brain-based learning challenge.

There are private tutors and specialized learning centers that target the unique needs of dyslexics. Many of these use an Orton-Gillingham-based approach, which is outlined in more detail in a later section in this appendix.

Homeschooling

Families often get frustrated with a school's inability to meet their child's needs and decide to homeschool. But many make the mistake of trying to re-create at home the same system of education that wasn't working. This is natural because it is what they are familiar with themselves. Most homeschool curricula they consider use the same grade-level focus that has previously failed their student.

A child is not a grade-level package. There are multiple skill strands within the broader subjects of reading, language arts, and math. A student's ability can vary widely, even across many grade levels, between skill strands within each subject. A dyslexic child who is chronologically a fifth-grader might have first-grade-level spelling skills, third-grade-level skills in written composition, the speaking and listening vocabulary of a high-schooler, and reading comprehension that matches that of their fifth-grade schoolmates. No pre-packaged curriculum can meet them where they are in each skill strand.

A student might have been physically or mentally absent when a concept was taught, it might not have been presented in a way in which they could learn, or their brain might not have been developmentally ready when the curriculum stated to teach it. It is time well spent to go back and lay a strong foundation by filling in gaps, as many concepts are prerequisites for later learning.

We work with many homeschooling families that have pulled their dyslexic student home because they were floundering in school despite supports provided. Many of these families work with us to create a reading and language-arts plan that specifically targets their child's exact needs instead of wasting their valuable time and energy on activities that are poorly matched to their child's current abilities. By backing up to the student's level and bumping up the time and intensity at this Just-Right Level, we often see one-and-a-half to three years' gain in reading in six to twelve months.

This is accomplished by using regular homeschool time in targeted ways, not by hours of homework or extra tutoring. Imagine having that time free to devote to family or personal interests. Appropriate levels of instruction, practice, spaced review, and assessment are built into the programs we choose for the student. Reteaching is provided if needed. Targeted supplemental practice sheets are often available for topics such as commonly confused words and reading skills.

Drawing upon my experience and advanced training with Orton-Gillingham, Davis Dyslexia Correction, and several approaches for addressing underlying cognitive functions, I'm able to assist families in figuring out which components are appropriate for addressing their child's unique needs. Only an educational psychologist or similarly qualified professional can provide an official dyslexia diagnosis. I can guide a family down the path to which interventions are likely to fit whether or not they pursue an official diagnosis. Because many students simply need early intervention, a Path to Success Personalized Learning Plan from Wings to Soar Online Academy can fill the gaps and have the child reading at grade level for less than the cost of getting an official diagnosis.

Addressing Underlying Developmental and Cognitive-Function Weaknesses

Many students have underlying developmental or cognitive-function weaknesses that need to be addressed in order for them to get the most benefit from any remediation. These include weaknesses in memory, attention, processing speed, auditory processing, visual tracking, and the ability to cross the midline of the body so both sides of the body work together in a coordinated manner.

Neuroplasticity of the Brain – IQ Is NOT Static!

The traditional "wisdom" in special education has been that intelligence quotient (IQ) remains static over time. This is true *only without* specific mental training to strengthen underlying cognitive functions. Since most schools have embraced the traditional wisdom, they don't expect to see much change in IQ with special education; therefore that is usually the result they get.

In contrast, marked improvement often occurs for kids who participate in programs that focus on strengthening underlying cognitive processing. This is accomplished by exercising the necessary neurological pathways through targeted use, spaced repetition, and review of the new skills at gradually increasing difficulty levels. Educational psychologists who are not used to seeing changes in IQ scores are often quite surprised at the retest scores of kids who have been through these kinds of programs. Naturally the best results are reached when parents and students stick with the schedule and the amount of time required, and properly do the exercises provided in the programs.

There has been much recent neuroscience research showing the plasticity of the brain. This means that the brain can and does change depending on how we use it. The neural pathways we use repeatedly become stronger. The body coats the neuron with a fatty-acid layer in a process called myelination. This insulates the neuron so the electrical impulses that carry messages travel through it more efficiently. This is why omega-3 and omega-6 fatty acids are so important to our physical and mental well-being. They are essential for this myelination process.

The saying "Use it or lose it" is true in the case of neural pathways. The neural pathways we do not use atrophy, or dissolve, over time. The brain rewires itself to be most efficient for the decisions and actions that occur on a regular basis. For example, if you need to be out hunting for your food, that requires different neural pathways than if you need to hunt for nuances in text.

Whatever it is you practice is what you become proficient at doing. The areas of your brain that you use frequently become more efficient over time. Practice really does make perfect, or at least leads to mastery. It is important to practice correct techniques for whatever you're learning. It is very difficult to unlearn bad habits. The brain physically needs to rewire itself in order to unlearn something.

Neuroplasticity research shows that the brain can and does change with focused effort and practice. This gives hope to those struggling with dyslexia and other learning challenges. The phrase "neurons that fire together wire together" can help you remember what you are giving your child during those repeated practices.

Strengthening Underlying Cognitive Skills

The approaches I overview below work on strengthening underlying cognitive skills (mental-processing skills). They are based on current neuroscience research that shows that neural pathways that are repeatedly trained and strengthened are more efficient. While these approaches are less established as interventions for dyslexics, for many struggling learners, training with one of these approaches is even more important than academics. It lays the foundation of more efficient neural wiring, allowing all of the thinking and learning using that neural wiring to be that much more effective. Although not documented specifically for dyslexia, they are documented interventions for many conditions that a dyslexic person can also have.

Wings to Soar offers BrainWare SAFARI, Cogmed Working Memory Training, and Fast ForWord. These online programs develop cognitive processing. Although a trained professional oversees a student's progress and meets with them periodically via phone or webcam, the cost is much lower than going to a professional's office for one-to-one sessions. The online programs we offer are often much more affordable given that a computer can provide much of the intervention and the trained coach is only needed for oversight. Online programs provide the added bonus that time can be spent retraining the brain wherever there is internet access rather than requiring travel time and expenses.

BrainWare SAFARI

BrainWare SAFARI incorporates the latest neuroscience and decades of proven clinical approaches to cognitive-skills development into an engaging video-game format. It is supported by published research showing improvement in cognitive skills of two to four grade levels on average after 10 to 12 weeks.

By strengthening the cognitive skills that are the most necessary for performance in school, work, and life, BrainWare SAFARI builds learning capacity and effective thinking. BrainWare SAFARI is designed to provide the inherent engagement and motivation of a video game. It includes 20 games that develop and strengthen 41 cognitive skills that fall into six categories:

- Attention
- Memory
- Visual processing
- Auditory processing
- Sensory integration
- Logic, reasoning, and planning

BrainWare SAFARI trains the underlying skills that enable students to learn and demonstrate learning. Building the cognitive skills that are critical for learning so that each student has the capacity to succeed in school and in life results in:

- Greater attention and focus
- More efficient thinking pathways
- Better recall of information

- Improved ability to grasp new concepts
- Faster completion of work
- More self-confidence
- Greater attention to detail
- Improved ability to work independently
- Stronger visualization skills
- Improved mental speed
- Fewer careless errors
- Less frustration with difficult tasks
- Improved ability to follow instructions
- Improved problem-solving ability

Although BrainWare SAFARI does not teach reading, math, or other academics, a student's ability to learn these subjects improves as their underlying cognitive skills improve. So does their ability to take in, apply, understand, and retain information. Because of this we recommend that most of our students at Wings to Soar complete BrainWare SAFARI to boost their learning in all other areas. Frequency and intensity of usage are critical for cognitive growth. The recommended usage is 30 to 60 minutes, three to five times per week for 10 to 12 weeks.

Cogmed Working-Memory Training

Cogmed Working Memory Training (Cogmed) is an online solution that specifically targets working-memory skills. Cogmed exercises help increase the number of pieces of information the memory can retain at one time. It specifically targets working memory, which results in improved attention. Students have often been misdiagnosed as having ADHD when working-memory challenges are actually the primary cause of their difficulties.

An improved working memory prepares students for being more successful in school and in life. Areas in which improvement can be seen include:

- Paying attention
- Being less distracted
- Taking initiative
- Completing assignments
- Being self-directed
- Getting started and finishing tasks
- Working more independently

Some students experience dramatic improvements, while for others the improvements are more subtle. But even being able to hold on to one more piece of information while completing a task can make a huge difference in efficiency and reducing frustration. Cogmed's research shows that 80 percent of people who use this program see significant results.

The beauty of this program is that it continually adjusts to challenge the learner so that they are constantly stretching their abilities and improving. At the end of each session kids are rewarded with a fun game that is directly tied to their success in the training session. Kids love seeing their progress rewarded!

Wings to Soar offers Cogmed (for enrolled students) as an eight-week intervention with game-based training exercises delivered four times a week in 35- to 45-minute sessions and a weekly 15-minute coaching session with a certified Cogmed coach.

Fast ForWord

Fast ForWord is a more intensive intervention for students who have a significant gap in reading, issues with auditory processing, and two or more of the following problems: memory, attention, processing speed, and sequencing. Targeting underlying cognitive functions directly gets at the root of the reading struggle that must be addressed for any reading intervention to be effective. Following two foundational modules that specifically build these underlying cognitive skills, the program moves on to specifically build language and reading skills. Fast ForWord is very effective at improving auditory processing and is a dyslexia intervention tool. Many scientific studies have been conducted to document this program's effectiveness.

For some students, reading interventions tried previously haven't addressed some of the real underlying issues. What we've found is that auditory processing is often at the root of the problem for these students. This means that the brain has difficulty understanding the sounds and the words coming in and knowing what to do with them. Fast ForWord adequately addresses the auditory-processing problem for many students. Some need recommendations from an audiologist for continued intervention.

Does any of this sound familiar?

- Significant challenges with spelling
- Lost in many everyday conversations
- Environments with a lot of background sound make problems much worse
- Rhyming words has always been difficult
- Difficulty distinguishing one sound from another
- Trouble with listening comprehension and reading comprehension
- Trouble following multi-step instructions
- Other interventions have not resolved the problem, so there might be more than just dyslexia that needs to be addressed

If so, the problems the student is having could be resistant to intervention because there are multiple components of cognitive functions and processing that are affected. The problems with reading are just one symptom, so we need to address all those interlocking layers.

Fast ForWord assigns a few of the game-based learning activities each day. Our recommended protocol is 30 to 50 minutes, five days per week. This program constantly adjusts to the student's level so that their brain is challenged at the level it's ready for at any given time. Students are neither bored nor over-challenged, which often lead to frustration.

If Wings to Soar recommends Fast ForWord, it will usually be in conjunction with other reading and spelling interventions. After we review the child's and family's needs, we put together a Path to Success Personalized Learning Plan to help the child thrive. In addition to the programs, families also get monthly private coaching to help them ensure they're using the programs most effectively for their needs. The coaching provides the support so families can create a learning environment and structure in which the child can successfully thrive.

Here are the results we see with our students at Wings to Soar who use Fast ForWord as part of their dyslexia intensive intervention (when used as recommended):

- A one-and-a-half- to three-year reading level gain (and often more) over the course of a school year in this program
- Greater independence
- Learning in other content areas becomes easier
- Special-needs students are able to move into more mainstreamed classes and aren't held back by their challenges
- Improved brain-processing efficiency
- Long-term gains as students' brains are rewired

We've had over 50 students work through the Fast ForWord program in the past few years. Those who practiced regularly made some excellent gains. It's meant to be a 30-, 40-, or 50-minute daily protocol, five days per week. Most students who are good candidates for Fast ForWord benefit from one to two years in the program. Students who participated at least 80 percent of the recommended time saw one-and-a-half- to five-year gains over the course of a year. Obviously those who did not follow the program didn't do as well. As with any intervention, you have to actually use it as recommended to get the results desired.

Other Cognitive-Skills Training Programs

Two other cognitive-skills intervention programs that have solid supporting research and with which I have personal experience are the National Institute for Learning Differences (NILD) and Feuerstein Instrumental Enrichment (FIE). These are both much more expensive given that they are delivered one to one or in small groups with highly trained specialists. Both are excellent programs.

There are many other programs that claim to address underlying developmental skills and cognitive functions, such as Learning Rx, Brain Balance, National Association for Child Development, The Well-Connected Brain, and Brain Gym® International. I do not have adequate personal experience with these programs to be able to recommend them, although I have heard positive anecdotal reports from happy users. If they have research studies documenting their results, I have not personally read them, since Wings to Soar focuses on online interventions rather than in-person options.

Always conduct your own research before proceeding with any program, especially if there is a substantial financial investment. Many programs make broad and sweeping claims that are beyond the scope of what current research reveals. I recommend considering programs that have multiple published research studies in respected, peer-reviewed journals to find the best program for your child.

Be sure to follow the protocols of any program in which you choose in invest your time and money. If your child does not put in the necessary time to do the work, they won't get maximum results.

Orton-Gillingham

What Is Orton-Gillingham?

If you are exploring dyslexia intervention options, you have likely heard of Orton-Gillingham. The core Orton-Gillingham principles are considered by many to be the gold standard in phonics-based dyslexia intervention. Many programs have been developed that use the core Orton-Gillingham principles. I'll overview some of these programs after I introduce the principles.

Samuel Orton and Anna Gillingham did their research in the 1930s. Samuel Orton brought together that era's neuroscience research and the scientific principles of remediation. Using these he formulated a set of teaching principles and practices for children struggling with what we now know as dyslexia. Scientist and psychologist Anna Gillingham worked with Dr. Orton at Columbia University, training teachers and publishing instructional materials on his method. Combining this with her own model of the structure of American language, she co-authored *The Gillingham Manual: Remediation Training for Children with Specific Disabilities in Reading, Spelling, and Penmanship*, first published in 1935. Today the eighth edition is still used as the basis for many Orton-Gillingham training courses.

An Orton-Gillingham approach involves direct, systematic instruction in phonics. As stated previously, 80 to 90 percent of dyslexics have weakness in phonological processing. Orton-Gillingham-based interventions are explicit in teaching the sounds, rules, and principles of phonics. This approach employs multisensory strategies for using as many neural pathways and making as many connections in the brain as possible.

The Basic Orton-Gillingham Session Format

The basics of an Orton-Gillingham session involve similar steps no matter which program you're using:

1. **Phonogram reading:** The tutor shows the student a card with a phonogram on it. A phonogram is a letter or group of letters representing a sound. The student is expected to pronounce all the sounds they currently know for that phonogram. (Some programs teach all the sounds that a phonogram makes at once. I shy away from these programs because I think they unnecessarily complicate things for students by having them learn much less frequently used patterns early on. I've spent over a decade researching word frequency myself. I prefer to focus first on the most commonly used patterns. They can learn all the rest of the phonemes, spelling patterns, and sounds that go with them gradually over time.)

2. **Phonogram spelling:** After reviewing all the known sounds on each card, for all the phonemes currently being worked on, the tutor turns the cards around and pronounces a sound. The student must write all the ways they know to spell that sound.

3. **Read phonetic words:** The student reads isolated words using a target phonetic pattern or patterns. Then they read some words that provide a mixed review of the target patterns recently studied.

4. **Spell phonetic words:** The tutor says a phonetic word that the student has learned to read. The student repeats the word and pronounces each sound that comprises the word as they write it.

5. **Read controlled sentences:** The student reads sentences that contain the target pattern and reviews previously learned words.

6. **Write sentences from dictation:** The tutor dictates sentences with focused patterns for the student to sound out as they write.

7. **Read longer controlled passages:** The student reads longer passages of controlled text that contain only the words and patterns that have already been studied.

Many dyslexic individuals can go a long way in their eye-reading skills with the direct, systematic, explicit, multisensory Orton-Gillingham instruction. This work should ideally take place five times per week to provide the necessary spaced repetitions that build the neural pathways in the brain. This kind of remediation takes time. Students should start to improve within 25 to 35 hours of deliberate and intentional work using almost any remediation approach.

Orton-Gillingham Intervention Options

Many programs have been developed to help implement the basic Orton-Gillingham approach outlined above. Barton, Wilson Reading System®, SPIRE, Slingerland®, Lindamood-Bell, and Project Read are all Orton-Gillingham phonics-based approaches. They all require both a fair amount of training and quite a bit of time with an experienced instructor. Costs can add up quickly, since working with a tutor two to four times a week is best. In some areas the Scottish Rite or 32° Masons offer free or low-cost traditional Orton-Gillingham tutoring for those who qualify.

Barton is the most common Orton-Gillingham-based approach that parents use at home with their children; though it is fairly expensive to purchase and can be time-intensive for the parent. If you want to go with this option, purchasing your first kit from their website provides ongoing support. Remaining levels can often be purchased used. There are a total of 10 levels, but many families drop out about halfway through the program because the process takes such a long time and gets boring for both the parent and student. All About Reading is a somewhat less intensive program based on Orton-Gillingham that you can use at home with your child.

Sometimes, with training, a parent can effectively do Orton-Gillingham tutoring themselves. However it often works better for someone else to serve as tutor, especially in the student's teen years. Kids need the parent to be their cheerleader. They don't want to show their weaknesses to Mom and Dad; rather, they need their approval. Sometimes parents from two different families take the training, then each can tutor the other parent's child(ren).

As a trained Orton-Gillingham tutor, I was excited to discover some quality Orton-Gillingham-based computer programs that I could offer through Wings to Soar including Reading Horizons and Nessy. MindPlay and Lexia are not explicitly Orton-Gillingham-based, but they follow the same important core principles. These online programs allow students the necessary time to work independently. They also provide progress monitoring, reteaching, and built-in reinforcements or incentives. They are much more engaging than earlier software that used Orton-Gillingham approaches. We get results much faster with far less complaining when students use a combination of these programs than I ever got in my many years of one-to-one traditional Orton-Gillingham tutoring or using a single program online.

For the cost of a few tutoring sessions your student can get a year of access to several of these online options. The student can do 45 to 75 minutes of structured practice each day, put together by experts and presented in an engaging, interactive manner. The programs do not involve a lot of time with a parent or tutor because the programs themselves provide immediate feedback. This allows the parent to remain the cheerleader. Online programs are great because the computer provides instant impartial feedback, and there is no person to get mad at. Online programs keep an objective log of both the time spent and the results obtained. They tweak the program to provide needed teaching and additional practice if needed. They move the student ahead when a predetermined proficiency level is reached. They offer spaced repetition, ongoing reassessment, and review when needed. These programs have allowed Wings to Soar to help many more struggling students through occasional, targeted support; corrective coaching; and check-in sessions rather than intensive one-to-one tutoring.

In short, the drill and practice that's needed to form the neural pathways in the brain doesn't necessarily need to be done with a human. There are greater learning gains, less emotional stress on the parent-child relationship, and better use of the student's time and parent's dollars by using the power of the internet.

Orton and Gillingham defined *multisensory* as reading it (visual), writing it (kinesthetic), and saying it out loud (auditory). Triggering all these senses and modalities at once cements the connections in the brain. The more diverse the connections, the better the brain can access that same information later and the more solidly that information is cemented in long-term memory.

The more senses a student can repeatedly use, the better. Therefore I take the multisensory experience beyond what Orton and Gillingham suggested with "read it, say it, write it." I developed a list of more than 75 fun, multisensory activities to make learning more engaging and tap in to even more diverse connections in the brain. I provide this list as a reference in appendix D. If a dyslexic child can retain and access information through a different neural pathway than a non-dyslexic child uses, isn't that still learning?

Davis Dyslexia Correction

I had made good progress with one of my early tutoring students using the basic Orton-Gillingham approach, but we were hitting a wall. Not knowing what else might be out there, I started contacting every tutoring program I could find, and discovered the Davis Dyslexia Correction method. It was completely outside the box, which of course appealed to me. I knew that the folks at Davis must be either completely off the wall or they were on to something.

I told my tutoring student's family, "I really don't know if this is the right thing for her, but I think you should at least talk to them." They took my advice and did the initial assessment, followed by the 30-hour, one-week intensive program. The result was a two-year gain in her reading skills! The family no longer needed my services, and I was very happy for them.

Still, I was skeptical. The Davis folks told this family that a phonics-based approach isn't necessary, which is the opposite of what Orton-Gillingham teaches. I wondered if she would have made the same progress without the solid phonics foundation Wings to Soar had given her prior to the Davis intervention.

Later that summer, while working at my dad's educational store, I discussed the Davis approach with my dad. A customer overheard the conversation and chimed in, "My son went through that program six months ago. He's doing phenomenally. I highly recommend it." That confirmed it. I decided to start training in the Davis Dyslexia Correction method.

I practiced my new skills with some of my clients, and it made a big difference to those who embraced the mental strategies I taught. One family drove from Ohio to Wisconsin to spend a week working with me to help their daughter. She gained about two grade levels in that week alone. Even more exciting was reconnecting with this family a year later at a homeschool convention in Ohio. While I was there, the girl asked permission to finish reading the last several pages in her book before moving on to something else. The gains from her training had served her so well that she wanted to read for pleasure! Her dad couldn't thank me enough.

The Davis Dyslexia Correction method began with Ron Davis, who is dyslexic. In his research he came up with a list of words that triggered what he called "disorientation" in himself. He kept track of the words that caused him trouble as he read. He then asked other dyslexics to keep track of their own "trigger words," assuming they'd likely be different for each individual. However, he noticed many of the same words on all the lists. Many of the words were also on basic sight-word lists, but not all of the sight words were trigger words. The words that were trigger words were not easy to picture. For example, verbs and nouns like *jumping* and *apple* are easy to visualize in the brain. Trigger words do not connect with ready, mental images. Try to mentally picture words like *the* and *that* and *and*. Dyslexics freely place any of these non-picturable little words in the "blank frames" in the mental movies their minds are constantly creating, which triggers disorientation. Ron Davis found 217 words for this dyslexic trigger-word list.

Davis's "mental movie" parallels the material-reasoning strength that the Eides discuss in *The Dyslexic Advantage*, and is part of what I referred to in chapter 2 as the visual-spatial flip-side strength. According to Ron Davis, dyslexic infants learn to wrap their mind's eye around unfamiliar 3-D objects to better identify them. As they are introduced to the 2-D world of reading, they visualize a moving picture in order to understand what they are reading. A non-dyslexic also creates images in their mind; however, a dyslexic requires this constantly changing mental movie to make sense of the text.

The Davis approach is twofold. During a 30-hour, one-week intensive Davis course, the facilitator first orients the individual by helping them create a mental strategy for choosing to place the mind's eye "on point." This means that the mind's eye is looking down at the same angle that the student's actual eyes are looking. This position allows the mind's eye to function in the world of 2-D print. The individual chooses when to do this, and "says" to the mind's eye, "I need you to do a reading- or math-type 2-D task, so I need you to be on point." When the mind's eye jumps, which it will, the student uses that mental strategy to bring it back on point while they need it to work in that 2-D mode. When the mind's eye is on point, it sees the same thing that the physical eyes see.

In solving real-world problems, the best strategy is having the mind's eye look at the problem from all angles. If the student uses their natural 3-D approach when trying to read, it's not going to work so well. This is why being able to choose when to switch between their natural 3-D mode and the learned 2-D mode is so empowering for a dyslexic.

The second part of the approach begins with learning the Symbol Mastery process through a series of exercises to "detrigger" the alphabet and punctuation symbols. Then the student and parent are taught how to model the trigger words in non-air-hardening clay. They work through about a dozen of the 217 trigger words during that week. They continue together with the rest of the list at home. They create 3-D models of the dictionary definitions of the words and shape the words themselves. These are not words that are easy to picture. They model the dictionary definition so that the student can point to each part of their 3-D model and tell someone the definition from the model. Then they take a mental picture of their model and the word, and state the definition referring to their mental picture of the model.

The word *the* means "that one which is here or which has been mentioned." I have modeled the word *the* so many times with clients that I have it memorized. My image has a person that represents me pointing to a little ball and then a speech bubble behind me containing another little ball. It works for me; and I can point to all the parts of the definition within my clay model.

The purpose of Symbol Mastery is to have the student use their creativity through the active process of creating in clay. They create a 3-D visual representation for themselves that their subconscious can then recall and put into their mental movie in place of the blank. Now the word can add to the meaning rather than trigger disorientation, which happens when the mind's eye jumps off point to try to resolve a confusion.

The Symbol Mastery website (www.symbolmastery.com) has examples of each trigger word modeled in clay to help with ideas if the student and helper are stuck. But the individual's creative process of developing their own clay model is very important to this practice, so don't be tempted to just copy the examples. For easy words, this Symbol Mastery process can take five to ten minutes. For harder words it can take 15 to 25 minutes. While this may seem an inefficient use of time, it can be critical for finally mastering the trigger words that have tripped them up for so long. These words are also very high-frequency words, making up nearly half of the words seen in written English.

If your child continually struggles over these trigger words, taking the time to do this process can be worth it. I think the Symbol Mastery modeling component is the most effective part of the Davis program. The Eides, in *The Dyslexic Advantage*, also refer to this strategy, but view the rest of the Davis approach with some skepticism.

The Gift of Dyslexia, which should be available in your public library, offers detailed descriptions of the Davis program. Ron Davis donated copies to every library in the US in hopes that other people would be helped as he was. If the student has more difficulty with handwriting, math, and attention than with reading, his other book, *The Gift of Learning*, is the better choice.

Davis's books describe the program in enough detail that you can try to do it yourself. My caution about using only the book without a trained facilitator is that if that level of intervention fails, you shouldn't be tempted to write it off as another program you tried that didn't work. There is a reason that Davis requires 400 hours of training and practice to become a licensed facilitator.

A Davis program with a licensed facilitator isn't cheap due to the extensive training required and the substantial one-to-one time needed, but it can be worth it. It's not uncommon for students to end up with two-year gains during that initial week. They then continue to make incremental gains as they model the rest of the trigger words with the help of their parent at home. Like any program, there has to be student and parent buy-in to do the mind work necessary and to put in the time to do the follow-up exercises in order to get successful results.

Dyslexics are often better whole-word readers, with strong visual memories. Another strategy Davis uses that can benefit them is called Sweep-Sweep-Spell, which I mentioned in the reading fluency section in chapter 4. It helps solidify in the brain what the spelling looks like in a left-to-right fashion. This practice is designed for a student and a helper to perform for up to 10 minutes per day. Use a text level that is fairly easy for the student but includes some words they don't automatically recognize. One word at a time is uncovered. Then the student, if they are able, reads it and moves on to the next word. If they can't immediately read the word, they sweep their eyes across it to see if they recognize it. If not, they sweep their eyes across from left to right again. If they do not get it at this point, they spell through the word one letter at a time. Then the helper provides them with the word and they continue on. This exercise is purely for building word recognition.

When reading a narrative text, the Davis Picture-at-Punctuation strategy is used. Students are asked to form a mental picture of what they have just read at each punctuation mark, and to reread it if they cannot do so. This reinforces that reading involves gaining meaning from the text. Once the single-sentence level is easy and automatic for the student, this strategy can also work at the end of a paragraph, and they gradually build to picturing what they've read at the end of a page or section. This lays the foundation for identifying what's important while paying attention to the details. It builds the student's ability to summarize, using their strength in forming mental images.

Although I completed the first three weeks of Davis training, I cannot claim to be a licensed facilitator because I didn't complete the additional four weeks of required supervised practice. I do know enough about both Davis and Orton-Gillingham to speak intelligently about both programs, as well as to advise when a student might be a particularly good candidate for the Davis approach.

What characterizes a good Davis candidate? Someone who:

- has strong visual-spatial and 3-D picture-thinking skills
- is age nine or older
- is intrigued by the approach, committed to giving it a try, and thinks it might help them
- is willing to use the mental tools they are taught
- frequently has difficulty with the 217 trigger words, which usually are learned as sight words in kindergarten through second grade
- has an adult who will spend the time doing the ongoing follow-up work with them

Neither the International Dyslexia Association (representing the Orton-Gillingham approach) nor the Davis Dyslexia Correction method recognize one another as being needed. I disagree with them both. Each system addresses pieces of the puzzle, at least for some dyslexics. For the 80 to 90 percent of dyslexics with weak phonological processing, an Orton-Gillingham phonics-based approach is very beneficial, at least for spelling, and most likely for reading as well. For those with strong visual-spatial skills – our 3-D picture-thinkers – some of the Davis approaches are beneficial. For those who overlap these two categories, which include many dyslexics, each approach has something to offer.

Orton-Gillingham deals with underlying weak phonological processing. It systematically builds the foundation and skills needed to tackle reading any phonetically regular word. Depending on which expert you read, between 80 and 97 percent of words in the English language follow phonetic rules.

Davis says students don't need to spend time working on this weak area of phonics because the Davis strategies work around it by tapping in to the student's strengths of 3-D picture-thinking and whole-word recognition. I think the Davis strategies are best suited to working with sight words, many of which are also dyslexic trigger words according to Davis. I think this portion of the Davis Symbol Mastery approach is the most usable for someone who is not a trained Davis facilitator.

In summary, we covered three major approaches to remediation. Some students can benefit from incorporating elements of all of these approaches:

- Addressing underlying cognitive functions
- Tackling the phonics – the sound-symbol connection – through Orton-Gillingham
- Using the 3-D picture-thinking strength through Davis to master troublesome sight words

Wings to Soar Custom Learning Plans

Addressing underlying cognitive functions first, or concurrently with other strategies, can enhance a student's learning potential whether or not their challenge is dyslexia. It can make any other intervention and/or academic learning more effective, and might be the best investment of your limited financial resources. Programs like BrainWare SAFARI, Fast ForWord, and Cogmed Working Memory Training are some of the programs overviewed in this appendix that strengthen these brain processes.

Dyslexics with strong 3-D picture-thinking abilities can likely benefit from some or all of the Davis approach. This is especially true if they have ongoing difficulty with the dyslexic trigger words, those high-frequency words that are not easy to picture. The Davis approach is not recommended before age seven, and age nine is the most expedient age at which to begin. If you suspect problems, intervene early with an Orton-Gillingham approach. For many, this is sufficient by itself. For those who need Davis, it will have laid the phonics foundation needed for spelling.

Please refer to chapter 7 to learn more about our approach at Wings to Soar. Many of our students experience a one-and-a-half- to three-year gain in reading within a single school year, often progressing a year or more in the first semester by simply following their Path to Success Personalized Learning Plan. As they get caught up to grade level, the rate of gain will likely slow. But as they continue using programs they have learned to love because they are successful with them, it is possible they can become advanced learners rather than strugglers. If you're going to do it, do it well.

If You're Going to Do It – DO IT!

No matter which intervention you choose, it takes time and many repetitions at a gradually increasing level to strengthen the neural pathways in a dyslexic person's brain. Use the recommended protocol. It's not fair to say that a program didn't work if it wasn't used in the way it was intended. Students need to put in the appropriate amount of practice each day or week over a period of time to determine if they are making the progress the program says they should. If you're going to invest in an intervention, make it a priority to do it and use it. This applies to any intervention or curriculum.

It has been my experience that students start seeing gains when they have used any of the quality programs according to protocol for 25 to 35 hours. The gains continue with consistent use and practice. Almost without exception, the only students who don't see substantial gains are those who dabble in the programs and don't consistently use them as directed.

Children who in the past have melted down because they were expected to work in material that was beyond their level may have developed this as a habit. They need to be expected to try as they work in programs that are at their Just-Right Level. A curriculum should still be challenging at times, but they need to learn that it is doable and be expected to push through. They can take breaks as necessary, but expect them to come back to doing the work. Most won't like spending the amount of time needed working on reading which has been difficult for them. To see the gains they have to put in the time doing whatever program is chosen.

Don't stop the intervention when your student has just gotten up to grade level. Continue until they are at least a grade above the target level to allow their brain to solidify the new skills. This puts the student on a firm educational path to success.

Whatever intervention you choose, make it a priority to put in the time and effort to allow your child to make the progress that is possible for them. If you're going to make the monetary investment in an intervention, also be willing to put in the time investment to follow through. If you're going to do it, do it well.

Appendix B

Leveling the Playing Field through Accommodations

Accommodations are changes to how a child learns. An accommodation "allows a student to complete the same assignment or test as other students, but with a change in the timing, formatting, setting, scheduling, response, and/or presentation. This accommodation does not alter in any significant way what the test or assignment measures."[1]

The strategies presented here are powerful ways to support students with learning challenges. They do not "dumb down" the assignment, but make it easier to do the work. These strategies even the playing field.

This appendix focuses on how accommodations can level the playing field for the dyslexic. Some teachers and schools require an official plan, which in the US is called an Individualized Education Program (IEP), to allow these types of accommodations. Other teachers recognize that presenting material and allowing access in different ways is just good teaching whether or not the student has a diagnosed learning disability.

(See appendix H, "Making Sense of Jargon," for the differences between differentiation, accommodations, modifications, intervention, and remediation.)

The following are things parents and teachers can do without the aid of a specialist or intervention program; however, accommodations alone will never help a dyslexic child grow into their fullest potential. For some students accommodations are merely short-term fixes, while more comprehensive *interventions* address the foundational skills necessary to perform the standard academic tasks required of them. Other students will continue to use accommodations, such as audio books and speech-to-text software, throughout their adult lives. These are productivity tools for professionals, not just for struggling learners.

Scribe, Voice Recorder, and Speech-to-Text

Many dyslexics are actually good at storytelling. They can be very talented, creative writers if they can get their ideas down. The frustration occurs when something gets in the way of those thoughts flowing out of them. Not all dyslexics have the challenge of expressing what is going on in their brains, but many do. This can be due to dysgraphia – difficulty writing by hand; other handwriting or spelling challenges; or any other subcomponent skill that is not yet automatic.

I had a mom say to me, "If my daughter writes the paragraph herself it's going to be about three sentences. But if I take dictation, she'll write a page." This statement reveals something very important about the daughter. It shows both her skill limitation as well as her intellectual capability. She may have weakness in fine-motor dexterity, spelling, or handwriting; however, her intellectual capability is far beyond the limitation of her weak writing skills. If she is asked to constantly work within the limitations of what her weak skills can handle, she will rarely experience her intellectual level or challenge herself. This doesn't do justice to either her weak or strong skills. It is all frustration, with no joy of accomplishment. When the mother accommodates for the daughter's weak writing skills, the daughter blooms into a creative, expressive child.

Scribe

Write or type for the student so they can focus on their verbal flow of ideas. Scribing takes stress off the creative process for students whose writing can't match pace with their flow of ideas. This strategy:

- Gets rough-draft ideas onto the page
- Allows stream-of-thought ideas to be captured so they can be further worked with, organized, and expanded on
- Focuses only on getting the ideas out and onto the page, not handwriting, spelling, or grammar
- Prevents dysgraphia/motor-planning issues from getting in the way

If appropriate, the student can copy what was scribed later. Here are two variations on the scribe theme:

- Scribe "dictation": Write or type what the student dictates with few or no cues or questions. Two options:
  - Get down the student's stream-of-consciousness first-draft thoughts without interrupting.
  - Use when the writing is at the final draft stage. Ask questions only if the dictation is not clear. Accept word choice, sentence structure, etc. Read it aloud back to the student and allow them to edit as needed. Think "secretary."
- Scribe with cueing: While writing or typing, ask clarifying questions to cue the student to improve meaning and communication without telling them what to say. Example: "What are the characteristics of the 'stuff' you talk about here? How can you describe this better for the reader so they'll know your meaning?"

Voice Recorder or Voice-Recording Phone Application

This is an alternate option if a partner is not available to scribe. The student or adult can later transcribe the recording to work with it further.

Speech-to-Text or Voice Typing

Dyslexics and dysgraphics who have difficulty getting their thoughts down on paper should become comfortable with speech-to-text or voice-typing software. Knowing that this software can dramatically increase an individual's ability to flourish and is a good productivity tool for anyone, dyslexic or not, can encourage your child to embrace this tool. Doctors and lawyers use this tool to save time and eliminate transcription errors. Vocalizing punctuation takes a little time to get used to, but it just takes some practice. Here are two options:

- Google Documents' "Voice Typing" tool
  - Simple speech-to-text tool
  - Can be used as early as elementary school
  - Included with free word-processing program
- Dragon® Naturally Speaking
  - A full-featured speech-to-text program
  - The software learns a specific voice, speech pattern, and rate of speech, so the student should be past puberty – when their voice changes, before using it.
  - Requires some patience to learn, so give it at least a month of good effort.

Although I am not dyslexic, I relate to the pain of being trapped by weak handwriting skills. I wrote the following poem as I reflected on my struggle in fourth grade to integrate all the complex skills required for writing.

Thoughts, sentences, and paragraphs,

Oh my!

And spelling, letter formation, spacing,

and capitals, too!

Periods, commas, and make it grammatically correct!

And this handwriting just might get the best of me yet!

If only my mom had known the strategy of being my scribe! If she had said, "Talk it out to me. You can copy it later," it would have saved struggle and countless tears.

Other Assistive Technology

- Predictive-text software, which fills in a possible word as you type
- Spell-check software, which suggests alternative spellings when it doesn't recognize what you've typed
- Grammarly® is a useful application for anyone, not just dyslexics, that runs on top of most other programs including email, social media, and Microsoft Word (but unfortunately not Google Documents as of this writing). It highlights text that might have incorrect grammar, usage, or punctuation, and suggests alternatives.
- Typing should be learned as early as possible, though most people don't have the "motor coordination or finger span to truly touch type until about seven or eight years

of age."[2] However, students even younger than that can practice letter recognition and begin learning where the keys are on a typing keyboard. When they are old enough to learn touch typing, the motor-muscle memory involved helps reinforce spelling without having to contend with reversal and handwriting issues. Typing programs include:

- ○ Touch-type Read and Spell is fairly expensive for a typing program, but it also supports an Orton-Gillingham phonics approach to reinforcing phonics for reading and spelling.

- ○ An inexpensive typing program I have experience with that uses games for practice is Mavis Beacon Teaches Typing.

- ○ There are many other typing programs available that work as well.

- Text-to-speech / audio books

  - ○ Voice assistant – ask Google or Siri a question and they provide an answer

  - ○ There are numerous inexpensive text-to-speech apps that allow you to choose between multiple natural-sounding voices.

  - ○ Audio books

    - Just as a blind student "finger-reads" using Braille, a dyslexic can "ear-read" while listening to audio books, allowing them to access texts that they can't yet "eye-read." This provides access to grade-level vocabulary and content so they don't fall further behind.

    - Dyslexics should be encouraged to build their ear-reading skills starting in elementary school, concurrent with separate work focusing on strengthening weak eye-reading skills.

    - By reading along with the highlighted words as they are read aloud in Learning Ally, Bookshare, RAZ-Kids, or any other program that has this feature, the student often improves their eye-reading ability while training their ear-reading. This provides access to grade-level vocabulary and content so they don't fall further behind.

- Digital audio texts that can be sped up allow students to train themselves to listen faster than at typical listening speeds. Gradually increase the speed by 10 percent increments. They can train to listen with good comprehension at up to three to five times faster than typical listening speed, bringing their ear-reading speed up to that of a fluent eye-reader.
- Sources of audio books
  - Mass-market audio libraries such as Audible
  - Many libraries carry audio books in various formats.
  - Digital audio libraries are available to individuals who are blind, physically impaired, or have a learning disability that impairs access to printed text. Someone qualified must sign a form affirming the individual does indeed have a disability.
    - Learning Ally has over 80,000 human-narrated audio books. Narration quality varies widely, as these are provided by volunteer readers.
    - Bookshare has over 500,000 titles using "high quality" text-to-speech for their recordings.

Classroom Accommodations

- A teacher or a skilled note-taker provides a copy of notes.
  - Allows the student to focus on using their strong listening skills while taking in the information, increasing their ability to absorb the main points, subpoints, and details of the lecture.
  - Don't expect the dyslexic student to arrange for a note-taker themselves.
- Permission to audio record the class for those who would benefit from hearing the material again.
- Use of a calculator
- Use of a multiplication chart or formula card

- Testing accommodations: alternate ways to demonstrate learning
  - Extra time: time-and-a-half is a fairly standard accommodation for those with learning disabilities
  - Scribe
  - Reader or recording of test

If your child has not had a formal diagnosis but needs accommodations to do their best on tests, I recommend going ahead with a formal diagnosis by their junior year in high school, especially if they plan to go to college. That way they can have the accommodations to level the playing field on the ACT and SAT tests. Any accommodations they qualify for in the final three years of high school will typically be used to determine what supports they receive in college as well.

Tools for Managing the Sensory Environment

- **Oral stimulus:** Sugar-free gum, lemon drops, suckers, and straws help students focus. Sour is a stimulus that helps the brain stay awake. For many people chewing has a calming, focusing effect.

- **Weighted vests, lap blankets:** Weight added to the shoulders or torso can have a calming, focusing effect.

- **Exercise/stability ball or wiggle seat:** Helps a child who always needs to be in motion.

- **Visual screen:** A room divider or science-fair display board the student can use as a visual screen and a place for posting schedules, notes, and reminders. It can prevent distractions while they're working, but don't impose it on the student or it may be perceived as a "cage of shame."

- **Headsets/headphones:** Cuts the upper sound register to help with focus, and filters other noises as well. They must cover the ears completely to filter out sounds. They do not work as noise filters when used without audio input, though similar items sold as "ear protection" do, as do earplugs. Earbuds generally don't cover the ear, allowing more external sound through.

- **Ambient sound:** Any smart-phone or tablet application that produces white noise or ambient sound works to block out distractions. Low-tech options are rain machines, fans, air conditioners, and other machines that hum. These can be distractors for some highly sensitive people, but for others they mask distracting noises. Natural white noise such as waves, gentle rain, and soft instrumental music can also work.

- **Ambient light:** Turn off the lights and work by a window or other natural light source. This has a calming effect. It can also have a cooling effect on hot days if the sun isn't pouring in the window, or a warming effect in winter if it is.

- **Timers**
  - Visual timers such as the Time Timer® provide a visual image of how much time has passed and how much time is left for the task the student set it for, and come in a variety of shapes and sizes from a watch to a tabletop size. This visual representation can be very important for students who have poor conception of the passage of time.
  - A kitchen timer does the same thing without the visual image, and is less expensive. Students who need extra time to transition from one activity to another can set it to go off a few minutes early.
  - Reminder software such as Google Calendar alerts the student to an upcoming scheduled task or appointment.

- **Intentional Breaks**
  - Students should take breaks as needed to use the bathroom, exercise, or just chill. Set a timer to cue to resume work.
  - Students should close their eyes from time to time to rest them from continuous computer use or to block out visual distractions while thinking.
  - Students should learn to take a few deep breaths and refocus when distractions occur.
  - A healthy snack every couple of hours helps maintain a steady blood sugar level.

Appendix C

Teaching Principles, Strategies, and Tools

Keep the following key principles in mind whether you are teaching, homeschooling, or providing remediation or homework support after school for your child. If you are providing homework support, you may not be able to control some of these.

- Celebrate your child's uniqueness and help them grow to their maximum potential. Help them discover and develop their unique strengths and abilities.
  - Encourage exploration of their personal passions such as sports, music, art, and academics of a particular nature. While schoolwork should not be ignored, it's appropriate to pursue personal passions, and this can be done from an academic perspective, making their relevance more apparent.
    - What is the history of the area of interest? How was it influenced by history? What influence has it had on history?
    - How is it informed by and how does it influence various scientific and/or technological areas?
    - What math does one need to be proficient in it?
    - What foundational skills are needed to pursue it?

- What means of communication are needed to learn about and/or share the passion? What languages? What tools?
  - When learning is seen as relevant to the student's areas of interest, they will persist even if it is difficult.
  - Being well rounded is often overrated. A person should spend 85 percent of their time on what they do best and hire out the rest.[1]
- You are teaching a child, not a curriculum.
  - Go as slowly as they need to, but as fast as they are ready to.
    - Back up to the student's actual level.
      - In every skill-based subject area, including math and all areas of language arts, place the student at the level at which they are actually functioning in each skill strand rather than where their grade level says they ought to be, even if that means going back many grade levels in a particular skill strand.
      - Wings to Soar Online Academy offers free Just-Right Level Assessments to help with this. Request these at www.JustRightLevel.com.
      - I've found that a level that is a slight challenge, but at which they can usually succeed when working independently, is best.
    - Gradually bump up the time and intensity of work on the struggle area.
      - Once at the right level, the student should put in whatever time and effort is needed working on each of the areas of weakness until they are caught up to grade level.
      - Allow them time to lay a solid foundation of core skills. Don't be so intent on their being caught up that you shortchange the needed time to fill in gaps in their learning and master the skill.
      - Plateaus are normal.
        - After a period of rapid skill development it is very common for learning to plateau a bit as the brain takes time to consolidate new skills.

- Review and reinforce during this time, and don't allow yourself to get discouraged by it.

o Focus on weak skills separately and provide accommodations for those weak areas during a complex task.

- If asked to do too much at once, the student will not have enough working memory available to perform the task at all.

- Short daily practice sessions on these components of the bigger task are important, and they can bring these skills to the point of automaticity so they don't take up additional working-memory space and hold the student back.

- Content can be reviewed while shoring up weak skills.

  o Example: Use spelling words that have already been learned for handwriting practice.

  o Example: Use topics from their other current schoolwork for practicing writing skills at their actual functional writing level.

o Most students should be exposed to content at their intellectual level using appropriate accommodations such as scribes and audio texts. If the weak skills are the only focus, the student cannot grow their knowledge base.

- New content should not be taught as part of an exercise for strengthening a weakness, which leads to frustration. Concurrently, yes; simultaneously, no.

- In situations in which extreme remediation is needed, it may be appropriate to set aside other disciplines such as history and science for a year to focus intensively on developing underlying cognitive skills, math, reading, and language arts.

o Be flexible and adjust to what the student's next growth step is at any given moment.

- Yes, there are skills that are important to be mastered and content to which they need to be exposed, but keep the focus on the student and what the next growth step is right now.

- Sure, they might have been able to tackle something much harder last week, or even an hour ago, but what can they do right now in their current mental, physical, and emotional state that will continue to move them forward?
  - Scaffold as much as is needed for success, but your goal is to build confident independence.
    - Recognize that the level of scaffolding needed can vary day to day and even hour to hour. The most consistent thing is the inconsistency.
    - Provide the level of support that is needed right now.
      - If you provide more than is needed they won't develop independence; provide less and they will become overly frustrated.
      - See the more extensive sections below on scaffolding strategies and tools.
- Multisensory practice helps make learning stick.
  - "The best way to remember something is to change it – to transform the information in some manner.
    - If it is visual, make it verbal; if it's verbal, create a diagram or picture of it.
    - Use plenty of lists, tables, graphics, and other devices so that you're not merely sponging up the subject matter intact as it was presented."[2]
    - For example, color-coding names, places, dates, and other categories is a helpful visual way to transform the information.
  - Explore different ways to engage as many senses as possible in learning.
    - Kinesthetic – they don't have to sit still or in a chair to learn. In fact many do better with lots of movement and creative body positions.
    - Tactile
    - Visual
    - Auditory
  - Plan for physical activity. Getting the student moving is important for their health, their brain, developing healthy activity habits for life, and both parent and student

sanity. Exercise stimulates the brain. "Aerobic exercise remodels our brain for peak performance."[3] Have the student tackle difficult subjects after an exercise break.

- Balance
  - I haven't found a scientific explanation for why it works, but balancing seems to help focus, and focus helps learning. It could be that maintaining balance forces both hemispheres of the brain to cooperate and work together.
  - Use balancing as a short reset break between other learning activities, or have the student recite a lesson while balancing.
  - Simple balancing activities
    - Stand on one foot
    - Stand on head
    - Toss a Koosh ball while balancing on one foot
    - Balance board
    - Sit on an exercise ball
    - Balance beam – a 2x4 on the ground will do
    - Jump rope
    - Ride a bike
    - Bounce on a trampoline
- Rhythm
  - Have the student chant what they are learning while they engage in a rhythmic activity.
  - Simple rhythmic ideas
    - Skipping
    - Bouncing on a mini-trampoline
    - Bouncing a ball or tossing it up and catching it
- Cross the midline of the body
- See appendix D for many more multisensory practice ideas well-suited for memorizing spelling words and other factual information.

- Make learning fun!
  - The more you can teach and review using games the better.
    - A student who resists a workbook page will likely happily practice the same skill (if it is at an appropriate level) in the context of a game, and for much longer.
    - Use games to provide cumulative and mixed review.
      - Cumulative games provide repeated testing in fun ways. Include material from recent lessons as well as review lessons.
      - Put information related to a topic on separate cards. Use card sets from various topics to play matching games for cumulative review.
  - Create a song.
  - Create a skit and act it out.

Sharing the products of one's creativity adds to the pleasure and the motivation to push through to excellence. Share them in our Dyslexia Outside-the-Box Facebook group, and then let your friends know they are there. If you choose to share something you found beneficial from some other source, please credit the source.

Scaffolding for Success

In chapter 6 I provided an example of how scaffolding can apply to one specific type of writing. The parent or tutor should provide various types of scaffolding to support the student. The following strategies are examples for getting started:

- Essential Questions
  - Ask leading questions that lead the student to an answer whenever possible. Questions should:
    - Be open-ended – they do not have a single, final, and correct answer
    - Be thought-provoking and intellectually engaging, often sparking discussion

- Be able to be answered using critical-thinking skills such as analysis, inference, evaluation, and prediction; cannot be effectively answered by recall alone
- Integrate transferrable ideas across disciplines
- Serve as the beginning of further inquiry
- Allow for more than just an answer
- Need to be revisited again and again[4]

○ Essential questions help stimulate stream-of-thought, facilitate development of ideas, draw out details, clarify ambiguous points, probe for elaboration, find examples, give perspective, connect relevance, and extend to implications. Example: "If you had to explain this idea to a space alien, how would you describe it?"

- **Partnering** – Be a fellow discoverer in the learning process by partnering. Don't play dumb, but instead model finding something new (think out loud).

  ○ Partnering helps with focus, follow-through, modeling "how to," attention, and scaffolding growing executive-functioning skills.

  ○ Two variations

    - **Partnering with cueing:** Verbalize your mental process. Be "in the moment": verbalize questions, internal talk, and mistakes. Backtrack when you hit a dead end, and cue the student to do the same. Partners need to communicate since they can't read each other's minds. Let the student determine the pace, always. Examples: "To me, 'stuff' means..." "What did you mean here?"

    - **Partnering-as-Peer:** Again, don't play dumb, but let the student determine the direction (or misdirection) and pace of the learning. Ask questions and give feedback, but be the sidekick and not the superhero.

- Feedback

  ○ **Verbal Feedback:** A key element of effective verbal feedback is limiting the quantity and scope of feedback at any one time. Decide beforehand what single concept you will give feedback on and how many comments you will make, then hold yourself to that. Frequent, focused feedback is much more effective than overwhelming with it all at once.

- This strategy helps with perspective, review, focus, foreshadowing, and identifying areas in which improvement has been accomplished or is still needed.
- Two variations
    - **Observation only:** Verbalize what you see/hear, but don't qualify it or critique: "I see you included two examples for this point but no examples for the next point."
    - **Observation with suggestion:** Add a suggestion to your observation but word it in a way that gives the student choices: "I see you included two examples for this point but no examples for the next point. I need an example to help me understand exactly what you're saying. What can you give me?"

○ Encourage the student to ask questions such as these to help them incorporate feedback:
- What was I told?
- Do I agree with the comment?
- What change(s) do I need to make to include the suggested ideas in my own words or by including quotations with citations?

○ Monitor performance against some standard of what is needed or expected using a detailed rubric against which the student can compare their output.

○ Correct student work and provide feedback to the student on the same day the work is completed. Prompt feedback is always best, as the brain consolidates what we have learned during the day while we next sleep. It can discard wrong answers and start to consolidate correct answers. That is why instant computer feedback is often preferable to worksheets that someone needs to find time to correct.

○ Have the student keep a log of their day so they and you know how they have spent their time.

- Have them jot down start and end times for each task.
- Compare their log to the time reported in progress reports provided by online programs, and to teacher feedback concerning student progress or incomplete work.

- **Check-In/Check-Out:** These are used to help a student focus on the day as a whole or a specific project or task.
  - Schedule check-ins and check-outs with your student *daily*. They are important and should be scheduled and not rushed.
    - Do a check-in at the beginning of the school day or project session.
    - Do a check-out at the end of the day or project session.
  - Check-ins/check-outs help with informal assessment of the student's mindset through structured feedback.
  - They help with reviewing what has happened, foreshadowing next steps, and organization.
  - Don't let the craziness and busyness of life get in the way.
  - Give the student (then yourself) a chance to have the floor for about three to five minutes to respond to the check-in/check-out question.
    - Some check-ins/check-outs are relevant to the day as a whole. Examples:
      - "How do you feel today?"
      - "Rate your day so far from one to ten, with ten being the best. Why did you choose that rating?"
    - Some check-ins/check-outs are specific to a particular project. Examples:
      - "What concerns you or interests you about this project?"
      - "How are you feeling about the project so far?"
      - "Use three words to describe this project and tell me why you chose those words."
      - "What would be a good way to know when this project is successfully done?"

○ Essential questions (see examples in the "Essential Questions" section above) can be used as needed.

○ Use successive check-ins/check-outs to evaluate a student's understanding of the project thus far.

○ Keep the lines of communication open. This is not a time for judgment.

- Don't use a check-in/check-out as a "teachable moment" unless the student is asking for help; it is a fact-finding mission.

- This is a time when the student knows they can say what's on their mind without getting a lecture. Respond to frustrations and concerns – no scolding!

- During check-out ask, "Is there anything we need to talk about?" Try not to become defensive about whatever they share. If there is anything you can do about the stressor, say, "Thanks for sharing with me. Here's how I will try to change that. Do you think that will help?" Then follow through and make the proposed changes. In later check-outs ask if they are helping the situation.

○ The daily check-in/check-out procedure helps avoid nagging while maintaining accountability for doing the work.

● Scaffolding for project organization and process

○ The prefrontal cortex of the brain that is responsible for planning, organization, and other executive functions is still developing until about age 25. Young people need adults to support them by modeling over and over again the processes for planning larger projects to help develop this part of the brain.

○ Rather than allowing the student to just "find their own way," ask cueing questions to help the student learn how to plan a project.

- Talk through the expectations verbally when beginning the project. Clearly define the scope of the project.
  - ○ What do you want to or are you expected to do or know?
  - ○ What is the expected structure of the project?

- What type of organization is appropriate?
- What needs to be included in this project?

- Map out a plan for completing the project as a whole and jot down the steps in words the student understands with visual cues if needed.
  - What tools and/or supplies do you need?
  - What are the phases needed for the project?
  - How should it begin? Conclude? What has to happen in between?
  - How much time do you need to allow for each phase? Be sure to allow time for multiple revisions.

- Ask about research: Where are you going to learn about it? Credible websites? Library? Interviews? Field trip?

- During each project work session, use questions such as these to cue movement through the process:
  - How do you plan to tackle this project task?
  - Where are you going to start?
  - What do you plan to accomplish?
  - At the end of the work session:
    - Compare what was accomplished to what had been planned.
      - What did you accomplish today?
      - How is the plan working?
      - What results did you expect by now?
      - If it isn't working as planned, what changes can you make to make it work better?
    - Adjust the timeline planned for the project and/or the pacing of the work.

- Start work on large projects right away. Allow the student to stop when they hit a wall. Resume work after an intentional break. Have them do a little each day. If momentum occurs, allow them to go with the flow.

- Focus on one thing at a time until satisfied that it's been addressed for now. Come back to it later if other relevant thoughts arise. If those thoughts arise in the middle of doing something else, capture them and put them in the parking lot to be dealt with later.

Teaching Tools That Assist Scaffolding

- **Visual Flowcharts/Agendas:** Hands-on flowcharts and agendas can be posted anywhere. They can be fun to make and use. These are essential for many students to help them organize their time and work flow.
  - Create colorful graphics or use pictures of your student doing various tasks.
  - Use Velcro® or flannel to post these images in a chart that shows the order of events.
  - Put cues on an agenda board instead of expecting the student to remember the steps of a task or the succession of tasks to be completed.
  - Use a check-off system as each step is completed.
  - Create a "task completed" section on the agenda board and have the student move the graphic there once the activity is complete. Review the board during check-out.
  - Include graphics that represent "free time" or "break time" or other kid-friendly activities that can be added to the agenda as incentives.
  - Agendas help organization, tracking the passage of time, cueing what lies ahead, accountability, planning, and buy-in.
- **Parking Lots:** This business-meeting technique (also useful in school and in life) keeps track of side issues so they don't get forgotten. Use sticky notes to write down questions and comments that come up while studying. Without disturbing the flow of the lesson, post the sticky notes on a board or wall – the parking lot. At a scheduled time, go through the parking lot and guide the student in organizing the notes to determine a course of action on the issues. Toss parking-lot notes as the issues are resolved.

- o The parking lot helps with partnering, visualizing, planning/cueing, reviewing, prioritizing, categorizing, and general organizing, and minimizes distractions.
- o Special uses for parking lots
  - **"Tag Team" Brainstorming:** Use different-colored sticky notes for each person for brainstorming ideas, words, etc. When an idea is written down (or scribed), the sticky note is put in the parking lot. Leave the parking lot up throughout the project.
  - **Word Banks** are like tag-teaming above, but the focus is on words that might be used in the project. All words are accepted. Those not useful will be weeded out during categorizing. As words are used they can be moved to a "used" group so they aren't used repeatedly.
    - o Example: How many different ways can *said* be expressed? There are dozens of ways. Look them up in a thesaurus. What are the different shades of meaning suggested by each word? Does one convey the volume, tone of voice, or emotion with which the idea is expressed? Which one is best here? Keep this word bank (perhaps in a file folder) and use it for every writing project. Add to it as new "said" words are learned.
    - o Make a big wall chart of terms that help the student or potential audience understand an idea.
  - **Categorizing:** Categorize parking-lot sticky notes into groups. The groups can help organize the planning or writing process, show relationships within the topic, create to-do lists, etc. The idea is to break down the parking lot into manageable, related sections.
  - **Prioritizing:** Sort the categories in order of priority.
    - o What's "nice" to know; what does the reader "need" to know.
    - o What needs to happen first, second, etc.
    - o What's a "big idea" and what are the supporting "little ideas."

- o Use bull's-eyes, target shapes, and other symbols to identify different priorities.
- For those who have trouble retrieving information from their personal memory, storing and organizing what is currently being worked on in a parking lot can provide faster access.
- There's an online version of a parking lot at www.note.ly, or google "sticky-note board" for more ideas.

- **Graphic organizers**
  - o A graphic organizer is a visual display that demonstrates relationships between facts, concepts, and ideas, and guides the learner's thinking as they fill in and build upon a visual map or concept diagram.
    - The student will likely need to be taught how to create and use graphic organizers effectively.
    - They can be used to organize the ideas, vocabulary, and concepts to be learned as the student takes notes while reading or in class.
    - If they are not provided by the teacher, parents can use them to help the student organize information in a different way to see the connections between ideas.
    - The website www.readwritethink.org provides some great free, interactive graphic organizers.
  - o **T-chart:** Use a diagram in the shape of a T to categorize using two criteria, one on each side of the vertical line of the T.
    - Pros and cons
    - What supports or helps an idea, and what takes away from or hurts it
    - What "is" and what "isn't"; what "works" and what "doesn't work"; what's positive and what's negative
    - Can be used when the student has trouble making decisions. Discuss the possible choices and ask questions to draw out the consequences of each choice by sorting them into "what I want" and "not what I want" sides of the T-chart.

o **Fishbone:** Use a fishbone diagram to organize sticky notes into "causes" (minor bones of the fish) and "effects" (ribs and spine of the fish) or relating details to big ideas.

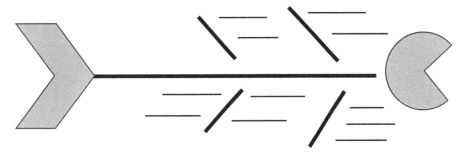

o **Venn diagrams:** These diagrams that use overlapping circles are useful when what is being organized includes both/and as well as either/or material.

● **Online/Electronic Tools:** Use internet resources and software to free up parent and student to interact with each other more. There are many free online applications that can help.

o Here are some quality online tools to check out:

● Google tools: Voice Typing in Google Documents, which is part of Google Drive; Calendar; Hangouts/Chat; Tasks; Keep

● YouTube/Google Hangout: video journal, video instructions

● Other useful online sites: www.Thesaurus.com, Visual Thesaurus, PEG Writing, Sticky-note Board (www.note.ly), Inspiration, Powtoon, ReadWriteThink, Cacoo, Edmodo, myHomework, Visual Timer

o A caution: be sure to practice using the application prior to working with the student so glitches don't interfere with the process. Or perhaps your student can help you learn how to use it!

o **Scavenger Hunts:** To build interest in a topic or sustain interest, use bookmarked sites or premade lists of internet resources (all media types) so the student can hunt for interesting tidbits. A scavenger hunt is exploratory, so include videos, cartoons, and sound clips rather than large collections of text-based information.

- Builds interest, innate curiosity, development of ideas, focus, detail, and brainstorming
- www.BrainPop.com is a great site for hunting
- Premade scavenger hunts can be found at www.educationworld.com/a_lesson/archives/scavenger_hunt.shtml

Thoughts on Foreign Languages

Learning foreign languages is often hard for dyslexics. Many dyslexics meet their foreign language requirement by learning sign language, which doesn't require dealing with the different sound-symbol system of another language. If they want to take a foreign language, I suggest a highly phonetic language such as Spanish rather than a language with complex spelling patterns and frequent irregularities like French (or English). In Spanish many words are similar to English ones, but it has a much simpler phonetic system. Avoid languages with different alphabets than the student's own language, such as an English speaker learning Chinese. Dyslexics do better in conversational and culturally oriented foreign-language classes that have less emphasis on reading and writing.

Appendix D

Expanded Multisensory Practice

When I began tutoring using Orton-Gillingham, I soon found that basic Orton-Gillingham can be boring. It can trigger the prime symptom that gets a child the ADHD diagnosis: failure to pay attention to a non-preferred activity that an adult is trying to get them to focus on. I started making practice sessions more interesting for my students by having them use more of their senses.

The multisensory practice ideas I developed provide a wide variety of practice. I encourage students to use them to practice particularly challenging spelling words. They can also help with memorizing anything that requires rote memory, such as math facts. These ideas use the different senses to engage as many diverse connections in the brain as possible, though the student is not likely conscious of how these additional sensory inputs enhance memory and retrieval.

The brain makes use of all the different modes of input; they provide more potential memory hooks to grab on to. By using multiple sensory channels, the brain can rewire around problem areas and tap in to strengths instead. Using a variety of multisensory inputs provides the needed repetition to get challenging words into long-term memory without boredom. Whatever other senses are being used, always pair them with saying out loud the word, letters, or facts being memorized.

These multisensory ideas should provide much of the needed practice for learning the spellings of rule-breakers, outlaw words, and any other words that cause trouble. They can also be used to learn phonetically decodable words and alphabet letters. However, the intent is to focus on sight words that need to be mastered by memorization rather than by patterns.

Research shows that it takes 60 to 75 repetitions of a word spelled correctly to build automaticity in long-term memory. I recommend using a Daily Basic 5 set (as explained below) for each word daily for the first two weeks after it is learned, and then weekly for the next month, to achieve 70 spaced repetitions of that word. Make sure the student does the practice correctly; it can take 600 to 2,000 repetitions to relearn a word that has been learned incorrectly![1]

For many students the more variety in multisensory practice you can provide, the better the words stick. Empower your student with choices of medium to use on any given day. If they have time to get out the sand tray or the Wikki Stix®, but not the clay or finger paint, make sure the choices offered are equally acceptable to the adult for this given practice time.

Include games to mix up the practice and make it more fun. Some game ideas are provided below. We tend to remember better when we associate what we are learning with having fun.

Wings to Soar Multisensory Practice Ideas

Daily Basic 5 Repetitions

Do the first four steps with each word:
- **Read** the word out loud, then spell it out loud while reading it.
- **Write** the word while spelling it out loud, then read the word. Vary the medium used, choosing from the ideas in the "Write" section below.
- **Go back to the model** (the printed accurate spelling of the word) and spell the word letter by letter, then read the word out loud.
- **Check** what you wrote letter by letter, then read the word.

The fifth step is to choose from one of these sections below: "Trace," "Visualize," "Kinesthetic," "Play with Your Food," and "Special Ideas." Vary the option chosen from day to day. With all variations, saying the word and spelling it out loud while writing it adds the auditory component. It also adds the feel of the mouth shaping the words and letters.

Write

For many of our dyslexic kids, picking up a pencil and writing seems like torture. But they do need to write the word in a way that leaves a memory trace of how to make the letters. They also need to be able to see how the word looks when it's written. Writing on a whiteboard, or dry-erase board, doesn't seem to carry the same aversion as picking up a pencil. Even writing on paper with a crayon in a couple of different colors, either one over the top of the other or right below it, mixes it up a bit, seems to be more accepted, and is a little bit easier than using a pencil. Using a chalkboard can work better than a whiteboard because the resistance of the chalk against the board provides sensory feedback to the brain that is not received from a dry-erase marker on a smooth whiteboard.

Full arm extension while writing on a whiteboard or chalkboard, or while sky-writing, uses larger muscles and therefore different neural pathways for gross-motor skills than those used for graphomotor, or handwriting activities; which in turn are different from those used in other fine-motor activities. Brain scans show that writing calligraphy causes different areas of the brain to light up than normal handwriting. An artistically inclined student might like to practice this way.

It's important to provide the brain simultaneous auditory, visual, and kinesthetic feedback. When working on a sight word, have the student spell letter by letter. When working on a phonetically regular word, have the student say the sounds as they write them.

Vary the writing step choosing from these options:

- Paper – with pencil, pen, crayon, marker, or colored pencil
- Whiteboard or chalkboard
- Manuscript, cursive, italic, calligraphy; lowercase, capital letters; and typing, so they get used to seeing the word in different ways
- Sand tray (a thin layer of colored sand in a shallow plastic container with a lid for easy storage)
- Sidewalk chalk or a wet sponge on a sidewalk
- Starting really big and then decreasing the size until it's tiny
- Rainbow colors, writing the whole word at a time with each color, either on top of each other or one after the other.
- On a zip-lock bag with finger paint inside (double bag it, and you only need a very small amount of finger paint)
- With the tip of a bar of soap, on the shower wall
- Use a new sight word in a sentence with one or more new phonetically regular words.
- Emphasize phonetically regular vowels using the Wings to Soar color-cue colors by writing the vowels in their special color:
  - short *a*=tan, short *e*=red, short *i*=pink, short *o*=olive, short *u*=plum
  - long *a*=gray, long *e*=green, long *i*=white, long *o*=yellow (or gold), long *u*=blue
  - /oy/=turquoise, /or/=orange, /er/=purple, /ow/=brown

In addition to reading it, hearing it, and writing it in the first four Daily Basic 5 practice steps, I encourage choosing from the "Trace," "Visualize," "Kinesthetic," "Play with Your Food," and "Special Ideas" options below for the fifth practice.

Trace

- On a printed model of the word
- On a handwriting model
  - finger or pencil
  - print or cursive
  - decreasing model sizes
- Using glue, trace a raised glue surface over the model. It can be allowed to dry and be traced over again on another day.
  - using glue, glue with sand, glue with yarn
  - using glitter glue, puff-paint pens
- On a tactile surface with the finger
  - on sandpaper, carpet, velvet, fake fur, corduroy, denim, silk, felt
  - on a table, leg, hand, arm
- Over Wikki Stix or a clay model of the word

Visualize and Other Visual Strategies

- Visualize the word spelled on an *imaginary whiteboard* just above and in front of the forehead. The helper asks:
  - What color is it?
  - Read the letters off the mental whiteboard.
  - What's the [second letter, third letter from the end, last three letters, etc.]?
- Draw a box around the shape of the word.
- Mark any irregular portion of the word.
- Color-code all the regular vowels.

Kinesthetic

- While balancing
  - using a balance board
  - on one foot
  - on your head
  - on a balance beam or 2x4
- While jumping: say the word, then spell (or sound) one letter (or sound) per jump
  - trampoline
  - jump rope
  - hopscotch
- While tossing a Koosh ball with a partner: The partner says the word and tosses the ball; the speller catches the ball and spells the word, then says the word while tossing the ball back.
- While tossing a ball up in the air: say the word, then say one letter per short toss, then say the word.
- While trying to keep a balloon aloft: try to spell the whole word before the balloon touches the floor.
- Sky-write the word using full arm extension, making sure to cross the midline of the body to activate both sides of the brain.
  - Writing the word in the water in a swimming pool imparts a different type of resistance during full arm extension than does sky-writing.
  - Sky-write or water-write while holding objects of different weights.
- Model the definition of the word in 3-D with clay, then make a model of the word in 2-D with clay ropes (see section on Davis Symbol Mastery in appendix A).
- Mix up letter cards for the word and then unscramble them.
- Make the word with rope or yarn across the floor – make it BIG.
- Walk along the large rope or yarn word as if writing the letter with your feet.

- Form the letters with your body.
- Spell the word using:
  - *Manipulative letters*: physical letters in the shapes of the letters such as alphabet magnets and tactile letters (such as Alphabet Avalanche™ from the Lauri company)
  - Scrabble tiles, letter dice, or alphabet blocks
  - Form the letters with pebbles, acorns, dry beans, etc.
- The partner spells the word with their finger on the student's back and the student tries to figure out what word was spelled.
- Write the word with a squirt gun against an outside wall on a hot day.
- Write the word in snow or sand using a stick.
- Walk out the letters that form the word in the snow or sand.
- Finger-spell using sign language.
- Explore the Braille version of the word.
- Use signal codes. See www.scouting.org/filestore/pdf/historic_signaling_new.pdf for more details.
  - Morse code
    - Have the code card in front of the student.
    - Tap, buzz, or flash the Morse code one letter at a time to the student.
    - Have them say that letter and all previous letters buzzed.
    - Have the student tap, buzz, or flash the Morse code for the word.
    - Use wigwag – Morse code via signal flags.
  - Turn it into a cheerleader's cheer, using pom-poms to wigwag it.
    - "S-u-c-c-e-s-s. That's the way we spell success!" is an example of such a cheer.
    - "T-h-e-r-e. First you're here and then you're there," can help the student learn which spelling refers to position.
  - Use semaphore flags.

Play with Your Food

You may actually want to encourage your student to play with their food!

- Spell the word with alphabet pasta or cereal.

- Spell it with M&Ms, chocolate chips, corn, beans, peas.

- Spell it with spaghetti.

- Write it in pudding – lick your finger if you spelled it right!

- Write it in finger Jell-O® before it sets.

- Cut out finger Jell-O letters with alphabet cookie cutters.

- Spell words in frosting on cookies or cake.

- Spell words with cookie dough (or use alphabet cookie cutters), bake, then say the words and spell them again before you eat them.

- Use your spoon or knife to write the word in your rice, gravy, or mashed potatoes.

- Anything that comes in a squeeze bottle, or can be dispensed in one, can be used to write words on food.
  - In syrup on your pancakes
  - In mustard or ketchup on your hot dog
  - In peanut butter or jelly on your bread

Special Ideas

Save these messier or more time-consuming ideas for a treat on a rainy day or for practicing particularly tough words.

- Shaving cream – squirt a little out and then write in it on the table

- Silly String®

- Finger paint

- Pipe cleaners

- Wikki Stix

- Clay: Roll out pencil-thick ropes and shape them into letters and words. You can color-code the vowels.

Increase Engagement with Word Sorts, Games, and Novelty

The first two girls I tutored would get really excited whenever I brought in something special to mix things up. "Yay, we get to do the sand tray today," they would say. For my third student, who was a more kinesthetic learner, I had to create more games and develop even more multisensory strategies to keep her engaged. I had to actively engage more of her senses. Reading the words off a printed list, as I'd been taught, worked with the first two, but it just wasn't working with her. Using the standard Orton-Gillingham drill format alone would get her through 10 words, then she'd buck me. But as soon as I made little word cards, worked around a simple track on a game board, or used any other game I could come up with, I'd get her to read between 25 and 40 words a session with no problem.

So I put all of the high-frequency words in a pattern on word cards and we played sorting games. Sometimes I had her sort 30 to 40 words into four patterns, reading them as she went. Sometimes we sorted by long and short vowels, or by spelling pattern. If we were working with a new pattern, we sorted by word families within that pattern. Sorting these words got her to think about the words and patterns more actively than if she were just reading down a list.

She also responded well if we played a simple game using a stack of word cards and a generic game board. She rolled a die and could move that many spaces reading one word per space. Then she aspired to read more words rather than dreading it. Using dice that had four, eight, ten, twelve, and even twenty sides added interest simply due to the novelty of the dice.

Providing her with unique games sparked her enthusiasm and provided her brain with different hooks for learning. She played the games unaware that in reality she was practicing and learning phonics and automaticity while creating a foundation for reading.

In another game we played, I put a cluster of outlaw words, which we defined as "words that break the rules together," on a card. She could move a number of spaces on the board that corresponded to the number of words she read correctly on the card. For example, she was excited to get the "-ind" card with *find, kind, wind, remind,* and *behind,* which allowed her to move more spaces than the "-ild" card which only had three words in the outlaw family: *mild, wild,* and *child.* We were building automaticity, and at the same time building awareness of how uncommon these outlaw family words were. It was also a creative way to move around the game board, and she became eager to read more words.

Appendix E

High-Frequency Spelling Patterns Worth Learning

The following lists contain all the words within either the top 300, top 500, or top 1,000 frequency of usage. I've chosen the frequency clusters to emphasize either just how few words there are in a frequency range or the priority to give the words when teaching them. The frequency range chosen for each pattern was selected to provide a manageable number of words and to provide an idea of how frequent a given pattern really is. These words should be priorities, as the top 1,000 words make up 90 percent of words used in written English. As the student encounters other words that use the patterns learned, encourage them to hook the new words to the core high-frequency words already provided here.

For more directed guidance for teaching these high-frequency patterns, as well as the rule-breakers and outlaw groups not addressed here, Wings to Soar offers the Wings to Soar Spelling Foundations curriculum I wrote based on my extensive research. The first level includes the following and other words that make up 71 percent of written English. The next two levels teach the remaining phonetically regular words that occur in the top 3,000 words.

Common long *a* vowel patterns

a-e

All long *a* silent *e* words in top 300:

came, same, name, make, take, made, place, page, change

There are many more long *a* silent *e* words in top 1,000.

ay

Used only at the end of a syllable.

All *ay* words in top 300:

way, may, day, say, away, always, today, play

All other *ay* words in top 1,000:

lay, stay, maybe, pay, played, playing, saying

ai

Used only in the beginning or middle of a syllable.

ain, *ail*, and *air* are by far the most common *ai* families

All *ai* words in top 500:

air

All other *ai* words in top 1,000:

rain, main, explain, train, hair, pair, tail, wait, afraid, raised

straight (and its variants like *straighter*)

is the only word that uses **aight** – memorize it!

There are other long *a* patterns that are NOT high-frequency patterns that are not worth

learning as phonetic patterns.

Common long e vowel patterns

ea   ee

Both *ea* and *ee* are very common patterns.

They can occur anywhere in the word.

There is no good rule for whether to use *ea* or *ee*,

so lots of practice with the high-frequency words in each group is needed.

Practice the words in each pattern together to reinforce which pattern to use.

ea words in top 500:

read, eat, each, easy, near, year, hear, really, sea, mean, means, meaning, leave

ee words in top 500:

see, three, need, between, keep, feet, tree, seen, green, seemed, needed, deep

Open syllable *e* in top 1,000:

be, me, we, he, she

Long *e* silent *e* in top 1,000:

these

There are other long *e* patterns that are NOT high-frequency patterns that are not worth

learning as phonetic patterns.

Common long *i* vowel patterns

i-e

All long *i* silent *e* words in top 300:

like, while, time, line, side, life, write, white, miles, five

There are many more long *i* silent *e* words in top 1,000.

igh

End of syllable or with a *t* after it.

igh words in top 500:

high, might, right, light, night

There are very few words that use the ***igh*** pattern

that are *not* high-frequency words.

y

y only makes the long *i* sound at the end of single-syllable words.

Open syllable y in top 500:

my, by, why, try

There are other long *i* patterns that are NOT high-frequency patterns that are not worth

learning as phonetic patterns.

Common long *o* vowel patterns

Single syllable open:

go, no, so

o-e

Long *o* silent *e* words in top 300:

home, more, before, those, whole

There are many more long *o* silent *e* words in top 1,000.

ow

End of syllable (or with *n* after).

ow as long *o* in top 500:

know, slowly, follow, following, own, below, show, shown, known, grow

oa

Only at the beginning or in the middle of a syllable.

oa in top 500:

road

oa in top 1,000:

boat, coast

The *oa* pattern is often taught early as a high-frequency pattern;
however, there are not many high-frequency words that use this pattern.

There are other long *o* patterns that are NOT high-frequency patterns that are not worth
learning as phonetic patterns.

Common long *u* / oo vowel patterns

There is a subtle difference between the long *u* and /oo/ sounds;
however, I have found that for most children, even dyslexics,
making the distinction is neither necessary nor particularly helpful.

u-e

Long *u* silent *e* words in top 300:

use, used

oo

Most common long /oo/ pattern, but not very common.

oo words as in *moon* in top 500:

too, soon, school, food, room, moon

ue

ue words in top 500:

true, blue

ew

ew words in top 500:

few, new

There are other long *u* patterns that are NOT high-frequency patterns that are not worth
learning as phonetic patterns.

Additional common vowel teams

ou as in *out*

Only at the beginning and in the middle of syllables.

Higher-frequency pattern than many long vowel teams.

ou as in *out* words in top 500:

out, about, house, without, around, found, sound, ground, round, outside

oo as in *book*

oo as in *book* in top 500:

look, good, looked, took, book, stood

ow

At the end of a syllable or with an *n* or *l* after.

(exceptions are crowd, browse, drowse, drowsy)

Top 500 **ow** as in words that sound like *cow*:

how, now, down, town, power

ea as short *e*

1/3 of the time **ea** makes the short *e* sound rather than more common long *e*.

These are all Old English words a common person would use.

ea as short *e* in top 500:

ready, head, instead, already, heavy

Six basic syllable types

Plus special endings that make up all English words

closed

Consonant closing off vowel sound causes short vowel sound.

open

No consonant closing off vowel in an accented syllable, vowel sound is long.

silent e

Makes the vowel that comes before it say its name, long sound.

vowel team

Letters together represent a long or variant vowel sound.

r-controlled

When a vowel is followed by an *r*,

the *r* controls and changes the vowel sound.

ar, ***or***, ***er***, ***ir***, ***ur***, ***ear*** (as in *earth*)

These are the r-controlled words that occur in the top 500:

ar

part, large, far, hard, car, start, dark

or

for, or, story, form, important, short, order, horse

er

over, under, after, never, her, every, ever

ir

girl, first, bird

ur

turn, turned, during

ear

earth, heard, learn, early

I don't choose to separate *air*, *are*, *ire*, and *ore* from the rest of their family, as the vowel sound is little affected by the *r* in these words. Perhaps "The second vowel helps the vowel 'stand up to the bossy *r*'" is an explanation that works if a child brings these up and wonders why we don't focus on them as r-controlled syllables.

sticky -le

consonant before the *le*

always sticks with *le* when you break syllables.

These are all of the **sticky -le** patterns:

–ble, -cle, -ckle, -dle, -fle, -gle, -kle, -ple, -stle, -tle, –zle

sticky -le in top 500:

little, example, table, able

If you want to keep the first syllable short you need to double the middle consonant if a single consonant sound is heard (except in -ckle and -stle, which already have a second consonant). Note: the *t* is silent in -stle.

Other phonetic-pattern words not in above patterns

Here are other top-300 phonetic-pattern words that do not fit one of the patterns above:

find, kind, most, old, all, ball, called, small,

going, being, until, also, into, begin, began, little

Here are other top 500 phonetic-pattern words that do not fit one of the patterns above:

saw, draw, because, boy, point, voice,

family, children, study, city, using, suddenly, probably,

happen, animals, yourself, themselves, myself, himself,

everything, everyone, someone, however

Adding Endings that Indicate How the Word Is Used

- Combination of root words and endings to indicate a plural or verb tense (stars, played, running)
- Add *s* or *es* to make a noun plural.
- Use an *s* for third-person singular verbs in the present tense. (He walks. She walks.)
- Add *ed* to indicate that a verb happened in the past.
- Add *ing* to form the present participle to show that an action is ongoing.
- Add *er* for a comparative adjective when comparing two things when "more" is not used to do this.
- Add *est* for a superlative adjective to indicate that it is the greatest extent of that adjective when comparing more than two things when "most" is not used to do this.
- common prefixes: *re-*, *un-*
- common suffixes: *-ful*, *-ly*, *-ment*, *-ness*, *-er*, *-est*, *-ing*, *-ed*

Wings to Soar Dictation Sentences for Spelling Placement covers all of these patterns to assess which words give a student trouble. The first 100 dictation sentences, which cover lessons 1 through 18 in Wings to Soar Spelling Foundations, allow us to assess short vowels, blends, open syllables, and silent *e* patterns, as well as 90 sight words. The words tested in these 100 dictation sentences make up over 60 percent of words used in written English. The next 18 lessons focus on common vowel teams and r-controlled patterns, as well as an additional 90 high-frequency sight words. By the end of this level a student will have learned over 71 percent of the words used in written English. All words covered in Wings to Soar Spelling Foundations are assessed in these dictation sentences. Request these and other free Just-Right Level Assessments at www.JustRightLevel.com.

Appendix F

Phonological and Phonemic Awareness Exercises

The point of all of the following phonological awareness activities is for the student to focus on and manipulate the sounds within words, *not* read the letters, symbols, and words. This skill is completely oral and auditory.

Short daily practice with these kinds of exercises at the preschool and kindergarten levels, and for any older student who is not yet strong in these skills, is very important. It can be in a five- to ten-minute practice session or casually incorporated as you go about life together. Phonological awareness is one of the best predictors of reading success, and therefore of success in school.

Rhyming

- Say a word and have the student repeat it. Then ask the student to say a word that rhymes with it (hat, cat, sat, rat, fat, flat).
- Say a pair of words and ask the student whether or not the two words rhyme.

Sound-Providing

- Say a word and ask the student what sound they hear at the beginning of it.

- Say a word and ask the student what sound they hear at the end of it.

- Say a word and ask the student what sound they hear in the middle of it.

Sound Categorization

- Ask, "Do you hear [specific sound] in [specific word]?" For example:

  o "Do you hear /t/ in *bat*?" (yes)

  o "Do you hear /t/ in *ball*?" (no)

- Ask, "Which word begins with [specific sound] in [two specific words]?" For example, "Which word begins with /b/ in *cat, ball*?"

- Say the target word and have the student repeat it. Ask, "Which one of these words has the **same beginning sound** as [target word]: [word 1, word 2, (word 3)]?"

  o For example, "Which one of these words has the same beginning sound as *hat*: *cab, had*?"

  o After the student has mastered two choices, proceed to providing three choices.

- Say the target word and have the student repeat it. Ask, "Which one of these words has the **same ending sound** as [target word]: [word 1, word 2, (word 3)]?"

  o For example, "Which one of these words has the same ending sound as *dog*: *pig, kit*?"

  o After the student has mastered two choices, proceed to providing three choices.

- Say the target word and have the student repeat it. Ask, "Which one of these words **does not begin the same** as [target word]: [word 1, word 2, (word 3)]?"

  o For example, "Which one of these words does not begin the same as *kid*: *dig, king*?"

  o After the student has mastered two choices, proceed to providing three choices.

- When the student has become good at the previous variation, use the following: "I will say three words. Tell me which of these words has a **different beginning sound**. Wait until you hear all the words before you tell me which word does not begin the same as the others." This is a slight wording change that means about the same as the previous "does not begin the same" (versus "different beginning sound"), but it's important for the student to become comfortable with both.

- Say the target word and have the student repeat it. Ask, "Which one of these words **does not end the same** as [target word]: [word 1, word 2, (word 3)]?"
  - For example, "Which one of these words does not end the same as *star*: *car, storm*?"
  - After the student has mastered two choices, proceed to providing three choices.
- When the student has become good at the previous variation, use the following: "I will say three words. Tell me which of these words has a **different ending sound**. Wait until you hear all the words before you tell me which word does not end the same as the others." This is a slight wording change that means about the same as the previous "does not end the same" (versus "different ending sound"), but it's important for the student to become comfortable with both.

Blending

For these exercises the student will need small manipulatives such as colored blocks, felt circles or squares, beans, or bingo chips, in six different colors, with two each of at least one or two colors. The student should eventually do these types of blending exercises without needing the manipulatives, however, the manipulatives are very helpful in the early stages.

Compound Words

- Say each pair of compound word segments (such as *cup * cake*), pausing between them.
- Have the student repeat the segments using a manipulative to represent each one.
- Have the student blend the segments by pushing the manipulatives together and saying the word as a whole.

Syllables

- Say each pair of syllables (such as *pic * nic*), pausing between them.
- Have the student repeat the segments, using a manipulative to represent each one.
- Have the student blend the segments by pushing the manipulatives together and saying the word as a whole.

Onset and Rime

- A *rime* is a vowel and what comes after it in a syllable. An *onset* is what comes before the vowel. If two words have the same rime, they rhyme.
- Say each onset and rime pair (such as *r * at*), pausing between them.
- Have the student repeat it, tapping a block for the onset and tapping again for the rime.
- Have the student blend the segments by pushing the manipulatives together and saying the word as a whole.

Segmentation

Sentences

- For this exercise the student needs a piece of paper and a pencil, or a whiteboard and a marker.
- Dictate a three- to five-word simple sentence such as:
  - "The man sat."
  - "Dan has a fat cat."
- Ask the student to make a dash for each word. The idea is for the student to distinguish words as distinct from sounds or syllables.
- A more advanced variation includes both single and two-syllable words. Each word should have a mark (not each separate syllable).

Syllables

Say each word and ask the student to repeat it, clapping and counting the syllables. If they have trouble hearing the syllables, have them put their hand beneath their chin and count how many times it drops as they repeat the word. The jaw drops with each vowel sound and each syllable has only one vowel sound.

Phonemes

Say each word and ask the student to repeat it, tapping and counting the sounds, and then saying the word slowly, sound by sound.

Deletion

Compound Words

- Say the target compound word and have the student repeat it. Then say, "Say [target compound word] again, but don't say [either the first or second half]."
- For example, "Say *hotdog*, but don't say *dog*." The student should say "hot."

Syllables

- Say the target two-syllable word and have the student repeat it. Then say, "Say [target two-syllable word] again, but don't say [either the first or second half]."
- For example, "Say *pumpkin*, but don't say *kin*." The student should say "pump."

Phonemes

- Say the target three- to five-letter word and have the student repeat it. Then say, "Say [target word] again, but don't say [single sound]."
- For example, "Say *ham*, but don't say /m/." The student should say /ha/ with short *a* sound.
- A more complicated example is "Say *stand*, but don't say /t/." The student should say "sand."

Substitution

Compound Words

- Say the target compound word and have the student repeat it. Then say, "Say [target compound word] again, but instead of [either the first or second half], say [replacement word part that makes another compound word]."
- For example, "Say *pancake*, but don't say *pan*, say *cup*." The student should say "cupcake."

Syllables

- Say the target two-syllable word and have the student repeat it. Then say, "Say [target two-syllable word] again, but instead of [either the first or second half], say [replacement word part that makes another two-syllable word]."
- For example, "Say *mitten*, but don't say *mit*, say *kit*." The student should say "kitten."

Initial Sounds (Phonemes)

- Say the target three- to five-letter word and have the student repeat it. Then say, "Say [target word] again, but instead of [single sound], say [another single sound that makes a real word]."
- For example, "Say *bag*, but instead of /b/, say /t/. The student should say "tag."

Final Sounds (Phonemes)

- Say the target three- to five-letter word and have the student repeat it. Then say, "Say [target word] again, but instead of [single sound], say [another single sound that makes a real word]."
- For example, "Say *ham*, but instead of /m/, say /d/." Student should say "had."

Mixed Practice

- Place three blocks or chips of different colors on the table.

- Say the first word to the student and have them repeat it.

- Then say, "I want you to change [first word] to [second word with only sound change]."

- Have the student change one block to another color to show which sound in the word has changed, and then say the new word.

- Here's one example sequence to work through: ant, ants, pants, pant, plant.

Appendix G

Challenges that Often Co-Exist with Dyslexia

Most researchers agree that difficulty with the sound-symbol connection is a key component of dyslexia. The angle taken by the International Dyslexia Association is that this difficulty with phonics is the defining characteristic of dyslexia. Some researchers also add to this definition visual and auditory processing, as well as cerebellar components that can include speech articulation and motor issues.

Several related conditions often occur along with dyslexia. The latest research has not yet determined whether these fall under the definition of dyslexia or are separate, but co-existing conditions. Either way, all of a student's challenges need to be taken into account to gain perspective on how that student learns best and how to intervene on their behalf.

The goal of this appendix is to provide a brief introduction to what some of these other conditions are, introduce you to terms that you might encounter if you seek a formal diagnosis, and point you toward the professionals who are best suited to help with the different challenges. The brief summaries of these related issues that follow are intended to point you to further exploration.

Language-Based Learning Disability

According to the American Speech-Language-Hearing Association, "The child with dyslexia has trouble almost exclusively with the written word. The child who has dyslexia as part of a larger language learning disability has trouble with both the spoken and the written word."[1]

The following chart provides an overview of the core language components an individual must use. Reading is the area directly impacted by dyslexia. Other challenges often related to dyslexia can impact any of the other core language areas and need to be addressed separately with the help of appropriate professionals.

LANGUAGE COMPONENT	Receptive Language (taking in meaning)	Expressive Language (sharing meaning)
Oral Language	Listening	Speaking
Written Language	Reading	Writing

A *language-based learning disability* includes a spectrum of difficulties connected to understanding and using both spoken and written language. Dyslexia is a language-based learning disability that specifically presents phonological-processing challenges. Other language-based learning disabilities include challenges with:

- Expressing ideas clearly
- Learning new vocabulary words
- Understanding questions
- Following directions

- Understanding and retaining details
- Reading and comprehending material
- Learning words to songs and rhymes

The effects of a language-based learning disability can be wide-ranging, and students with a language-based learning disability can have difficulties with any or all of these skills:

- Listening
- Speaking
- Reading
- Writing
- Spelling
- Math
- Social skills

Many students with language-based learning disabilities also have weakness in one or more of the following executive functions:

- Attention
- Memory
- Organization
- Perseverance
- Self-regulation[2]

While most people think of articulation issues when they think of a speech-language pathologist (also known as a speech-language therapist), any student experiencing the ongoing challenges of a language-based learning disability should be evaluated by and work with a trained speech-language pathologist to help with these underlying language weaknesses. If there are other language difficulties besides dyslexia, the student will continue to struggle with reading and writing until they receive help with the underlying language challenges, even if they receive appropriate intervention for the dyslexia itself. All aspects must be addressed in order, starting with the internal, executive functions, then moving to the language areas in general, and finally to reading and writing.

Specific Language Impairment

Like dyslexia, *specific language impairment* is another diagnosis that falls under the broad scope of language-based learning disabilities. Specific language impairment can affect both receptive and expressive language including:

- Grammatical and syntactical development (such as correct verb tense, word order, and sentence structure)
- Semantic development (such as vocabulary knowledge)
- Phonological development (such as awareness of sounds in spoken language and the sound-symbol connection)[3]

Dysgraphia

Dysgraphia means difficulty writing by hand. The International Dyslexia Association's "Understanding Dysgraphia" fact sheet states that handwriting and spelling struggles are central to dysgraphia. The author refers to challenges of writing thoughts on the page as being part of a separate challenge. Others disagree and refer to this as a subtype of dysgraphia connected with executive-function concerns. Terms such as *specific language impairment* and *oral and written language disability* are labels frequently used to describe written/oral communication issues.[4]

See chapter 5 for more about supporting students with spelling challenges, and chapter 6 for more about supporting students with writing challenges.

Processing Challenges

Auditory Processing

The inability to differentiate sounds, or *phonological awareness*, is the root of the dyslexic's struggle to use the sound-symbol system (phonics) in reading and spelling. Difficulty with rhyming words is a common indicator. While some students simply lack phonological awareness, others have an *auditory processing disorder* that affects more than phonics.

An auditory processing disorder is not the same as a hearing problem. The American Speech-Language-Hearing Association states, "Auditory processing disorder refers to how the central nervous system uses auditory information."[5] Auditory processing disorder has symptoms that overlap many other challenges, and can be properly diagnosed only by an audiologist. In auditory processing disorders, any physical impairment to the auditory "hardware" has been ruled out, but the brain still has trouble processing the "signal." So while the individual's actual hearing is just fine, their brain has trouble making sense of the incoming auditory information.

An audiologist's diagnosis of *central auditory processing disorder* (also known as *auditory processing disorder* or *auditory processing deficit*) may include impairment in one or more of the following listening tasks:

- **Sound localization and lateralization:** the ability to locate the source of a sound and from which side of the body it came. This is important for safety; for example, locating where the sound of a car is coming from and where a barking dog is.

- **Auditory discrimination:** the ability to distinguish one sound from another. *Phonemic awareness* – the ability to notice, compare, and distinguish separate sounds in words – is a skill vital to reading. Kids with auditory processing disorder struggle to understand how different sounds work together to form words. For example, distinguishing between *seventy* and *seventeen*, and *free* and *three*, is difficult.

- **Auditory pattern recognition:** the ability to distinguish similarities and differences in the patterns of sounds.
- **Temporal aspects of audition:** the ability to:
  - sequence sounds (understand and recall the order of sounds and words)
  - integrate a sequence of sounds into words or other meaningful combinations
  - perceive sounds as separate when they quickly follow one another
- **Auditory performance decreases with competing acoustic signals:** difficulty perceiving speech and other sounds when others are speaking or another noise is present.
- **Auditory figure-ground discrimination:** the ability to pick out important sounds from a noisy background. Kids with auditory-processing challenges are overwhelmed by situations in everyday life because they can't filter out the background noise. Paying attention is incredibly difficult. They become overwhelmed and tune out or shut down as a coping mechanism.
- **Auditory performance with degraded acoustic signals:** difficulty perceiving "a signal in which some of the information is missing."[6]
- **Auditory memory:** short-term and long-term abilities to recall information presented orally.

Children with auditory processing disorder can have difficulty with:
- Understanding spoken directions and instruction
- Many aspects of oral communication, including expressing emotions, answering questions, and discussing ideas[7]
- Spelling, reading, and written expression[8]

Treating auditory processing disorders usually involves a three-pronged approach:

- **Change the environment.** Help the student take in the sound better by speaking more slowly, offering assistive listening devices, moving them closer to the teacher or away from distracting background noises, or minimizing other noise so they can focus attention on the important message.[9]

- **Strengthen other higher-order cognitive skills to compensate,** such as language, problem-solving, memory, and attention skill. The student should take responsibility for their listening success through active listening and problem-solving.[10] This will also aid with oral communication including expressing emotions, answering questions, and discussing ideas.[11]

- **Remediation of the auditory deficit** can involve computer programs and/or in-person therapy sessions. It needs to target the specific auditory challenges the individual faces.[12] At Wings to Soar we offer Fast ForWord, an online program with good results in helping students with auditory processing disorder.

Visual Processing

Optimally functioning vision includes three layers that might need to be addressed: sight (eyesight or visual acuity), visual efficiency (eyes working together properly), and visual information processing.

If a student is having reading problems, start with a routine eye exam to assess the physical health of the eyes and eyesight. If there is a physical problem with the sharpness or clarity of eyesight, it will be addressed with eyeglasses or contact lenses.

However, a student who has 20-20 eyesight can have visual processing challenges if their eyes are not working together efficiently. "Sight merely refers to eyesight or visual acuity. Vision refers to seeing, processing, and responding to visual information."[13]

A comprehensive vision exam with a developmental optometrist or ophthalmologist will assess visual efficiency, which includes how well the eyes:

- Fixate – look
- Follow – track
- Fuse – eye coordination
- Focus

Vision therapy exercises (lasting three to twelve months) might be recommended to help the six sets of eye muscles work together to make reading more comfortable. The College of Optometrists in Vision Development website, www.COVD.org, is the best source for finding a qualified developmental optometrist who can properly evaluate and provide vision therapy to treat these kinds of vision challenges. The website also provides useful checklists and developmental timelines to help parents identify whether their child needs this more thorough vision evaluation.

Other visual information processing issues that vision therapists address include:

- Spatial perception
- Eye-hand-body coordination
- Visual memory
- Visualization

Vision conditions that can benefit from vision therapy include:

- Eye movement disorders
- Inefficient eye teaming – eyes not working well together
- Misalignment of the eyes
- Poorly developed vision
- Focusing problems
- Visual information processing disorders[14]

Dyslexia can co-exist with visual processing disorders. When that is the case, each disorder needs to be addressed separately. A joint statement issued by The American Academy of Pediatrics and the American Academy of Ophthalmology says that scientific evidence does not support vision therapy as a treatment for dyslexia and other learning and attention issues.[15] Both vision therapy and dyslexia intervention may be necessary. One will not fix problems corrected by the other.

See It. Say It. Do It., by Dr. Lynn Hellerstein, outlines more fully the "Developmental Model of Vision" summarized above and is an excellent resource for information about developing visualization and visual processing skills. Another resource, *Eyegames: Easy and Fun Visual Exercises,* by occupational therapist Lois Hickman and optometrist Rebecca Hutchins, provides at-home activities to improve vision. However, these activities alone are not sufficient if the child needs visual therapy.[16]

For students who have already completed vision therapy or for whom visual-tracking challenges are less severe, Wings to Soar offers Reading Plus and MindPlay, which both include training of left-to-right eye-tracking, fluency, and stamina for reading as well as other aspects of reading skill development.

Processing Speed

Individuals with slow processing speed need more time to complete tasks. Processing speed issues can impact:

- **Visual processing speed:** how quickly our eyes perceive visual information and relay it to the brain
- **Verbal processing speed:** how quickly we take in auditory information and act on it
- **Motor speed:** typically as it relates to fine-motor tasks
- **Academic fluency:** the complex interaction of visual-motor skills, often with verbal components as well

Some examples of how slow processing speed affects learning include:

- Difficulty processing spoken information fluently or automatically
  - Difficulty listening to a lecture and taking in everything
  - Difficulty remembering and being able to follow oral directions, especially when presented quickly or with multiple parts
  - Difficulty listening and being able to follow a class discussion
- Problems getting information written down
  - Problems taking notes in class
  - Problems filling in an assignment notebook
  - Problems finishing an in-class assignment
  - Not having time to finish a test within the time allowed
- Slower reading fluency
  - Difficulty completing assigned reading in class
  - Not having time to finish a test within the time allowed
  - Fatiguing or not being able to complete longer reading assignments
- Difficulty sustaining attention to a task, not because of innate attention issues but because the attention gets lost in trying to process a lot of information coming in rapidly
- Difficulty retrieving known information from long-term memory fast enough
- Difficulty completing almost any task (activities, assignments, tests, transitions) within a specified time period
- Difficulty keeping up in social situations because verbal and nonverbal information moves too quickly and needs to be processed quickly

Slow processing impairs routine, at-home activities as well, such as:

- Getting out of bed and getting ready in the morning
- Getting ready for bed at night
- Falling asleep

- Making everyday choices
- Eating slowly
- Completing personal care tasks such as brushing teeth
- Starting or completing tasks, such as homework and chores
- Recalling names of extended family and friends
- Remembering upcoming activities
- Awareness of the passage of time

The information in this section is summarized from *Bright Kids Who Can't Keep Up*, by Braaten and Willoughby, which provides further useful information about children who fit these descriptions.[17]

Executive Functioning Issues

Executive functioning issues are usually found in kids with ADD or ADHD, but they are also common in kids with dyslexia. The following is a list of executive functions found in *Late, Lost, and Unprepared* by Drs. Joyce Cooper-Kahn and Laurie Dietzel[18]:

- **Inhibition:** the ability to stop behavior, actions, or thoughts when appropriate. The opposite is impulsivity – the weak ability to stop from acting on impulses.
- **Shift:** the ability to move easily from one situation to the next and to be able to think flexibly enough to respond appropriately in the new situation
- **Emotional control:** the ability to use rational thought to regulate feelings and emotional responses
- **Initiation:** the ability to begin a task or activity. It also includes independently generating ideas, responses, and problem-solving strategies.
- **Working memory:** the capacity to hold information in mind for the purpose of completing a task
- **Planning/Organization:** the ability to manage current and future-oriented task demands

- **Organization of materials:** the ability to "impose order on work, play, and storage spaces"
- **Self-Monitoring:** the ability to monitor one's own performance and measure it against some standard of what is needed or expected

The article "Understanding Executive Functioning Issues" by Amanda Morin shows how executive functioning typically works:

- "Analyze a task. Figure out what needs to be done.
- Plan how to handle the task.
- Get organized. Break down the plan into a series of steps.
- Figure out how much time is needed to carry out the plan, and set aside the time.
- Make adjustments as needed.
- Finish the task in the time allotted."[19]

Performing almost any task involves some level of executive functioning. If working well, the brain can move through these steps in a few seconds, but simple tasks become a challenge when these skills are weak. Because every person has a unique combination of each individual executive function, someone who struggles can display any of the following signs:

- "Finds it hard to figure out how to get started on a task
- Can focus on small details or the overall picture, but not both at the same time
- Has trouble figuring out how much time a task requires
- Does things either quickly and messily or slowly and incompletely
- Finds it hard to incorporate feedback into work or an activity
- Sticks with a plan, even when it's clear that the plan isn't working
- Has trouble paying attention and is easily distracted
- Loses a train of thought when interrupted
- Needs to be told the directions many times
- Has trouble making decisions

- Has a tough time switching gears from one activity to another
- Doesn't always have the words to explain something in detail
- Needs help processing what something feels/sounds/looks like
- Isn't able to think about or do more than one thing at a time
- Remembers information better using cues, abbreviations, or acronyms"[20]

Young children do not have well-developed executive functions. These skills typically grow in the course of daily life through imitating the examples set by teachers and parents through the preschool, elementary, and middle school years. For students with learning disabilities, nearly all executive functioning skills need to be explicitly taught. Scaffolding with temporary supports is necessary until sufficient repetition occurs to build neural pathways. More and more of these functions become fully operational as the prefrontal cortex in the brain, which controls executive functioning, reaches full development between puberty and the mid-twenties. Concerns regarding executive functioning need to be considered in light of what is typical at a certain age range.

Parents should play the role of surrogate executive and provide supports during growth of these skills. Supports will need to be used many times to provide the repetition the brain needs to internalize the skills. The brain needs many repetitions to strengthen the neural pathways to make the executive function automatic. A few examples of supports are:

- **Verbalize each step:** Model the task and verbalize each step in the task as it is completed. Be concise and consistent. This creates patterns for the brain to follow in future actions.
- **Checklists:** Any task or routine that repeatedly causes frustration can benefit from using a checklist, and it is a simple way to foster independence. Children do best when each step is supported by simple written directions.
- **Visual reminders:** These are like checklists except they outline the task through pictures. Take a picture of the child doing each individual step of the task, then put the pictures in order on a page. Do this for any task the child has difficulty doing but

needs to accomplish. For example, "clean your room" is meaningless to a child with executive functioning issues, but seeing a picture of picking up toys, and another of folding clothes, and another of shutting drawers, and yet another of making the bed gives the child step-by-step instructions for everything expected of them for that task. Give each task its own page, and put the photos in plastic sheet protectors in a binder. Cue the child to use the binder when they are asked to complete a task.

- **Use questions:** Anytime you can use a question to cue the child to complete a task rather than telling them what to do, you are creating a scaffold for their brain to learn how to think about the actions they need to take.

- **A simple verbal cue:** For some kids, simple cues such as "What do you need to be ready to go out the door?" are adequate. Others might need the more substantial supports described above.

Attention-Deficit/Hyperactivity Disorder (ADHD)

"Attention Deficit/Hyperactivity Disorder (ADHD) is a brain-based disorder that results in significant inattention, hyperactivity, distractibility, or a combination of these characteristics."[21] Many learning disabilities, including dyslexia and ADHD, are "linked both to heredity (genetics) as well as to brain structure and function."[22] Estimates are that about one-third of kids with learning disabilities also have ADHD.[23] Dyslexics are not an exception.[24]

The Mayo Clinic provides a comprehensive list of ADHD signs and symptoms, but also points out that if the child's attention-related concerns do not occur both at home and at school (or with friends), the problem could be other than an attention deficit. Some of the ADHD signs and symptoms are:

- Difficulty paying attention
- Frequently daydreaming
- Difficulty following through on instructions and apparently not listening
- Problems organizing tasks or activities

- Forgetful and loses needed items, such as books, pencils, and toys
- Fails to finish schoolwork, chores, or other tasks
- Easily distracted
- Frequently fidgets or squirms
- Difficulty remaining seated and seemingly in constant motion
- Excessively talkative
- Frequently interrupts or intrudes on others' conversations or games
- Frequently has trouble waiting for their turn[25]

Help students with attention issues by minimizing distractions:

- Move the student away from distracting peers, open hallways, and open doors.
- Create a workspace for the student that limits visual distractions.
- Use noise-cancelling headphones to minimize auditory distractions.
- Use well-designed computer-assisted learning programs that stimulate attention, limit the current task at hand to only what's on the screen, and provide immediate feedback.
- For paper-and-pencil tasks, use blank index cards to form a frame that blocks out unnecessary information on the page.

Taking care of physical health can have an impact on attention issues:

- **Drink more water.** Because the brain is 80 percent water, adequate hydration helps many brain functions.
- **Watch "junk" intake.** For some children, attention improves with the removal from their diet of artificial dyes and preservatives, sugar, sugar substitutes, and caffeine. Also limit processed foods.
- **Adequate rest.** Make sure the child has enough rest to be at their best, since attention, as many challenges, worsens when the student is tired.
- **Exercise.** Getting oxygen flowing to the brain is important for attention and learning.

Many students diagnosed with ADHD are actually exhibiting symptoms of another, less widely diagnosed challenge. Working-memory deficits often get missed because they look a lot like attention problems.

Working Memory

Attention lets information be taken in. Working memory allows the brain to hold on to information long enough to process it and make sense of it. Many students with learning struggles have challenges with attention, working memory, or both. At the Harvard Learning Differences Conference it was noted that working memory, attention, and executive function are closely linked cognitive functions that are "interwoven in a complex system of neural networks [that] are crucial to the learning process."[26] This is one reason that working-memory disorders are often mistaken for attention disorders. On the flip side, many of the same supports that help improve attention disorders also help improve working memory and other executive functions.

Working memory involves the brain manipulating information in some way to make use of it. When too many pieces of information come at the child all at once, they can shut down, explode, or express their overwhelming anxiety in other ways. A computer has a working memory as well. When it gets too many bits of data across its circuitry, it slows down or can lock up. When that happens, the computer needs to reboot. It is no different for a child.

How do you know if your child has memory issues? A child can be constrained by their working-memory capacity if they:

- Are easily distracted when working on or doing something that is not highly interesting
- Have trouble waiting their turn, for example in a conversation or when waiting in line
- Struggle with reading comprehension and have to read through texts repeatedly to understand
- Struggle with problem-solving that requires holding information in mind; for example, mental math calculations

- Are inconsistent in remembering math facts
- Struggle with completing tasks, especially tasks with multiple steps
- Have difficulty remembering long instructions given in several steps; for example, following recipes, directions, or school/work assignments
- Struggle to understand the context in a story or a conversation
- Have difficulties when planning and organizing something that needs to be done in separate steps
- Have difficulty staying focused during cognitively demanding tasks, but attend well when cognitive demands are minimal
- Have difficulty integrating new information with prior knowledge
- When called on, forget what they were planning to say
- Have difficulty taking notes and listening at the same time[27]

These problems can all be related to working-memory issues! At Wings to Soar we offer an online solution that boosts working-memory skills. Cogmed Working Memory Training exercises help increase the number of pieces of information the memory can retain at one time. Students using Cogmed see improvement in areas that have previously been thought of as attention problems. We also offer Fast ForWord and BrainWare SAFARI, which address working memory and attention as a portion of the cognitive skills addressed, as well as the Mindprint cognitive skills assessment, which assesses attention and working memory along with eight other cognitive functions.

Procedural Learning

About half of dyslexics have trouble with step-by-step tasks called *procedural learning*. Weak memory skills are a part of procedural-learning challenges. For parents of primary-school-aged students this can be especially discouraging, as nearly all skills presented at these ages require regular development of processes and memorization.[28]

Examples of procedural learning and memorization are:

- Days of the week and month; seasons
- The alphabet
- Math facts
- All of the computational math skills such as addition, subtraction, multiplication, division, and fractions

Dyscalculia

Students with procedural-learning challenges often have dyscalculia (difficulty with math). The *Diagnostic and Statistical Manual 5 (DSM-5)* lists *dyscalculia* as an alternate term for *specific learning disability with impairment in mathematics* (diagnostic code 315.1). See appendix H for more on the *DSM-5* and other diagnosis and policy documents.

Common characteristics of dyscalculia include difficulty with:

- Counting
- Learning number facts
- Doing math calculations
- Measurement
- Telling time
- Counting money
- Estimating number quantities
- Mental math
- Problem-solving strategies[29]

Math Supports

Most dyslexics' brains are not wired well for rote memorization. Simply doing more work on the math facts and practicing them a little harder probably isn't going to improve learning without being more strategic and systematic. Make the patterns explicit.

Dyslexics need a different approach, such as using hands-on tools called *math manipulatives* and creating associations with pictures, stories, or music. Math manipulatives can make learning math both visual and tactile/kinesthetic. Saying or singing what you are doing simultaneously with any other practice creates auditory pathways. This multisensory approach is powerful in creating lasting connections in the brain by providing more than one option for accessing what has been learned. Playing games provides the repetitions needed to make new neural pathways permanent. And games are fun as opposed to boring flash-card drills. The "fun factor" makes the brain receptive instead of resistive.

Help with Learning Multiplication Facts

- Try to help the student learn the patterns on a multiplication chart rather than doing rote memorization. For example:
  - 0 times any number is always 0.
  - 1 times any number is always the number.
  - To get 10 times any number, just add 0 to the number.
  - To get 9 times any number, just take away 1 from the number and put your answer in the 10s column. Then put whatever amount you would need to add to this number to make 9 in the 1s column. For example, 9 x 6 = 54, so 5 goes in the 10s column, since it is one less than 6, and if you add 4 to the 5 that equals 9, so that's what you need for the 1s column.

- To multiply by 11, put the number you are multiplying by 11 in both the 1s and 10s columns until you get to 11 x 9.

- Many students can multiply or skip-count by 2 or 5, or can learn to do so.

● Have them fill in a blank copy of the multiplication chart using these principles:

- Skip-counting by 2s and 5s brings the student to 7 fact families; they can fill in 7 of the 0-11 fact families. That leaves only 36 of 144 cells they have not filled in.

- If they learn to skip-count by 3s and 4s, they can fill in all but 12 cells.

- Because of reciprocals, such as 7 x 8 is the same as 8 x 7, there are only six facts for which they need to develop visual illustrations or drill until memorized.

- Once they realize how much they have already learned, it makes learning the remaining facts much less daunting.

● For most kids, multiplying by 6, 7, 8, and 9 is the hardest. Given that the visuals really help the explanation, I'm just going to send you to www.easycalculation.com/funny/ tricks/6-10-finger-multiplication.php for a cool finger-trick strategy that works for all of these.

Tips for Factoring

Factoring is breaking down a number into the series of numbers that were multiplied together to get it, and is used in algebra or when working with fractions. The easiest way to factor is to do a series of repeated divisions on a calculator, noting how many times you can divide by each number.

● If a number ends in 5, divide by 5 until it no longer ends in 5.

● If a number ends in 0, 2, 4, 6, or 8, start by dividing by 2.

- Continue doing this until your answer does not end in one of these numbers.

- Next try dividing by prime numbers 3 and 7. A prime number is one that can only be formed by multiplying itself by 1.

- Once this has been done, what is left are other prime numbers.

Focus on Real-World Math Skills

Sometimes no amount of multisensory strategies, graphic organizers, or length of time spent drilling charts works. Some students are not wired to ever master the math facts; their strengths lie elsewhere. If that is the case, a calculator is the solution. The goal for math is to understand when and how to use addition, subtraction, multiplication, division, and fractions. Memorizing the fact charts is not the goal.

The typical curriculum for teaching math requires pages and pages of practicing long computation problems to near perfection. If your student has to complete long-hand computation of problems, doing them on graph paper, with squares of the appropriate size for the student to fit one number in each square, can really be a life-saver for many students who struggle with keeping columns of numbers in line. Alternatively, turn lined paper sideways and use the lines to keep columns straight, putting one number between each pair of lines.

When is the last time you got out a piece of paper, wrote down a math problem, and solved it by showing your work long-hand style? Perhaps you do if you still keep a paper check register rather than using online banking; however, do you compute the problem in your head or use a calculator? The same logic applies to a dyslexic child. It may not be worth the frustration and energy to force them to perfect skills they will always struggle with. Rarely (if ever) will it be necessary in real life to use these skills.

Students should learn the concepts in math that are actually applicable to real-world living. Encourage them to do problems that apply math skills to real life. I'd rather have a child understand which buttons to punch on a calculator to solve practical problems than memorize a multiplication table and show long-form division without understanding how to use them in real life. If they really need to figure out sales tax in a store or the best value for a box of macaroni and cheese, they will most likely have a device with them that can do that. What they really need to understand is what type of calculation is needed, how to punch in the equation, and whether the answer makes sense. For fractions, focus on the basic fraction skills you actually use in life for measurement and cooking.

Many dyslexic students actually thrive when they get to higher-level math even if they aren't proficient in long addition, subtraction, multiplication, or division. If they can follow the logic required in the higher math to understand the sequence of steps they need to punch into a calculator, they will not be held back from pursuing higher-level math. If they are comfortable using the multiplication chart, even if they haven't fully memorized their math facts, they can still do the factoring they need in algebra.

Provide a student who has memory challenges, dyslexia, or dyscalculia with a reference resource for the necessary formulas to perform any needed calculations. This allows them to get on with *using* math rather than being penalized for not remembering a formula. In the real world we can look up formulas when we need them. A multiplication chart is another such resource that students should have access to while working on other math skills.

Highly Sensitive

Highly sensitive people are those whose nervous systems are more finely attuned to sensory stimuli. They are also much more sensitive to their own and others' emotions. While individuals who have *sensory processing disorder* can also be highly sensitive, being a highly sensitive person is not a disability; they just have a brain that is wired for a more highly attuned nervous system.

While a higher incidence of highly sensitive wiring among dyslexics is not documented, indications are that 15 to 20 percent of the general population is highly sensitive. If a person is both dyslexic and highly sensitive, it just means that their needs as a highly sensitive person must be addressed in order for them to focus on learning. Their higher sensitivity might contribute to distractibility.

A quality, free assessment regarding sensitivity can be found at www.hsperson.com. For more information read *The Highly Sensitive Person* by Elaine Aron or *The Highly Sensitive Person's Survival Guide* by Ted Zeff; both books are focused on adults who are highly sensitive. For a book that discusses highly sensitive children, *The Highly Sensitive Child*, also by Elaine Aron, provides insight and many strategies for parenting a child with this unique wiring.

If you suspect issues beyond dyslexia, I recommend reading *The Mislabeled Child* by Brock and Fernette Eide to prepare to make informed requests for further assessment, and possibly treatment, by the appropriate qualified professional.

Appendix H

Making Sense of Jargon

Parents and caregivers of dyslexics can become overwhelmed with information from medical, psychological, educational, and governmental organizations. While studies, manuals, videos, and websites may be interesting research for those with leisure time, parents and caregivers just don't have time to absorb it all, much less implement the latest technique or quote the more recent policy. Knowing how this well-intentioned data supports dyslexic kids is what is valuable – not the jargon.

Yet it is in the best interests of dyslexic kids that parents and caregivers know how the latest data – the benchmarks, policies, and legislation – impact dyslexic kids. Being armed with this data is critical to being an effective advocate.

Individuals with Disabilities Act (IDEA)

The Individuals with Disabilities Act (IDEA) assures equal access to free and appropriate education (FAPE) regardless of disability. It was first passed by the US Congress in 1975 under the name "Education of Handicapped Children Act," then in 1990 and again in 1997 and 2004 under the title IDEA.[1]

IDEA describes a *specific learning disability* as:

- **"Definition:** A disorder in one or more of the basic psychological processes involved in understanding or in using language, spoken or written, which disorder may manifest itself in the imperfect ability to listen, think, speak, read, write, spell, or do mathematical calculations.

- **Conditions included:** perceptual disabilities, brain injury, minimal brain dysfunction, dyslexia, and developmental aphasia.

- **Not included:** a learning problem that is primarily the result of visual, hearing, or motor disabilities, of mental retardation, of emotional disturbance, or of environmental, cultural, or economic disadvantage."[2]

IDEA: Read the Fine Print

Simply put, IDEA guarantees that "access to equal education" regardless of disability is assured. But buyer beware! IDEA does not define what that education looks like. Nor does it hold school districts to a common level of educational excellence.

Schools are typically required to adhere to "adequate yearly progress" as their definition of education. The sad truth is that the school district defines this term,

- not the parent
- not the therapist
- not the physician or psychologist
- not the special education teacher

Let me repeat: The school district and its board, administration, and helpful attorneys have the final say regarding what is "adequate yearly progress," although the recent US Supreme Court 8–0 ruling in Endrew F. v. Douglas County School District provides hope that districts will be held to higher standards for special-needs students.

Since the term is relative, it is essential to understand not only what your local school district deems "adequate yearly progress," but to be sober and painfully clear about the differences between their definition and your definition of "progress."

Diagnostic Criteria of Specific Learning Disorder

Released in May of 2013, the *Diagnostic and Statistical Manual, 5th Edition (DSM-5)* provides physicians, psychologists, and other medical and therapeutic professionals with a formal diagnostic description of *specific learning disorder* from a medical and mental-health perspective. The IDEA term is *specific learning disability*, which is used in the school setting. Be aware that not everyone sees *specific learning disorder* and *specific learning disability* as equivalent.

I include below a summary of the official diagnostic criteria used in the *DSM-5* for specific learning disorder to help you determine whether or not your student qualifies and could pursue specific learning disorder as a medical/mental health diagnosis. This diagnosis is made as part of a comprehensive clinical evaluation that takes into account developmental, medical, family, and educational history; school reports; and appropriate educational and psychological testing.

According to *DSM-5*, a specific learning disorder diagnosis requires that all four of the following diagnostic criteria be met:

- Difficulties in learning and using at least one of the following academic skills lasting six months or more in spite of quality intervention:
  - inaccurate and slow or effortful word reading
  - difficulty understanding the meaning of what is read
  - difficulties with spelling
  - difficulties with written expression
  - difficulties mastering math facts, number sense, or calculation
  - difficulties with mathematical reasoning

- Skills in affected academic area(s) are shown to be substantially below what is expected for the student's age on individually administered standardized tests.

- Difficulties start during school years, but the full impact is not seen until demand increases beyond what their limitation can cope with. Timed tests, quick turn-around times for longer written assignments, and heavy academic loads are examples of situations that may exceed the student's capacity, causing learning challenges to surface in a student who was previously able to cope.

- Must rule out other things as the cause of the challenge before giving a *specific learning disorder* diagnosis. Cannot be due to:

  o low intelligence

  o vision or hearing problems

  o other mental or neurological disorders

  o environment

  o not being proficient in the language in which instruction is provided

  o poor-quality teaching[3]

At first glance it seems a diagnosis of specific learning disorder is general in nature and not very helpful. However, if each academic area and sub-skill-set listed below is noted, the description can be useful for specifying types of skills in which the student is having difficulty. Don't just accept a general diagnosis of specific learning disorder without a list of the specific natures of the struggles.

The following are the specific diagnostic codes with the specific categories that can officially be used for that diagnosis:

- 315.00 specific learning disorder with impairment in reading:

  o Word reading accuracy

  o Reading rate or fluency

  o Reading comprehension

Some clinicians say dyslexia isn't an official diagnosis anymore. And they are right that dyslexia is not a major diagnostic category, but it is listed in the *DSM-5* as an "alternative term to refer to a pattern of learning difficulties characterized by problems with accurate or fluent word recognition, poor decoding, and poor spelling abilities." If the label *dyslexia* is important to you, ask the clinician to include "dyslexia" in the diagnostic report along with the official terminology.

- 315.2 specific learning disorder with impairment in written expression:
  - Spelling accuracy
  - Grammar and punctuation accuracy
  - Clarity or organization of written expression

Note that the term *dysgraphia* is not mentioned in the *DSM-5*, even as an alternate term.

- 315.1 specific learning disorder with impairment in mathematics:
  - Number sense
  - Memorization of arithmetic facts
  - Accurate or fluent calculation
  - Accurate math reasoning

Dyscalculia is listed as "an alternative term used to refer to a pattern of difficulties characterized by problems processing numerical information, learning arithmetic facts, and performing accurate or fluent calculations."

Differentiation, Accommodations, Modifications, Intervention, Remediation

Differentiation

Differentiation offers different *ways* for students to take in and demonstrate their learning. "Differentiating instruction means that you observe and understand the differences and similarities among students and use this information to plan instruction…Teachers offer students choice in their reading and writing experiences and in the tasks and projects they complete. By negotiating with students, teachers can create motivating assignments that meet students' diverse needs and varied interests."[4] Differentiation is not just for struggling learners; it tailors the learning experience to each student in a group. Providing choices allows the student to own their learning. To differentiate an assignment, the teacher provides:

- different sources of information
- various modes of information
- and/or different *products* to demonstrate learning, such as using presentations or posters instead of reading from a book or writing on paper

Differentiation does not allow for "easier" and "harder" ways to do the assignment; it gives students choices so they can pick the way that works best for taking in information and demonstrating learning. The result is students own the product and choose what they do best. Ideally the various types of information provided address visual, auditory, or tactile learning, and the product types allow students to choose presentation types that appeal to them.

Allowing students to obtain information from their choice of multiple sources, such as books, videos, and audios, is one part of differentiation. Examples of differentiating output include different learning products such as writing a newspaper article, a diary entry, or a dialogue to convey what a student has learned about their history studies. Additional ways to demonstrate learning when not working on writing skills, while simultaneously demonstrating content learning, include graphic presentations, putting on skits, and dioramas. However, it's important to be intentional about which skills each type of output develops and offer choices that meet the learning goals.

Accommodations

Accommodations are changes to *how* a child learns. The demonstration of learning by the student does not change. An accommodation "does not alter in any significant way what the test or assignment measures."[5] An accommodation "allows a student to complete the same assignment or test as other students, but with a change in the:

- Timing
- Formatting
- Setting
- Scheduling
- Response and/or
- Presentation."[6]

Examples of accommodations include:

- A student who is blind taking a Braille version of a test
- Taking a test alone in a quiet room
- Using audio texts instead of print
- Having someone read the test questions aloud
- Using a scribe or speech-to-text software so the student can record their initial ideas orally
- Providing a copy of the teacher's notes
- Providing extended time for tests

Scribes, partners, and printed/recorded material do not dumb down the work for the student; rather they model skills, create visual cues, and take away the logistical obstacles that prevent the challenged student from participating.

See appendix B for more thorough overviews of several common accommodations.

Modifications

Modifications are changes to *what* a child learns. A modification is "an adjustment to an assignment or a test that changes the standard or what the test or assignment is supposed to measure."[7] These are also sometimes referred to as adaptations. Since modifications change what the student is actually expected to learn, they should only be used when accommodations are not adequate to help the student function at grade level.

Modifications should rarely include skipping steps. Instead, modify the number of sources to be used, the number of supporting details required, and/or the length of the final report, and/or the method the student is to use to present what they have learned.

An example of a modification is a student who is only required to answer a subset of the total questions other students are expected to answer. Another example is a sixth-grader working on third-grade reading skills because that is the level at which the student is currently functioning.

Start teaching reading, writing, math, and any other skill at the level appropriate for the individual student. They will gain more from working on the skill at their level than by forcing them to work at grade level if they are not ready for that level of work. Back up to their actual functional level, but gradually bump up the time and intensity of this work so they can eventually catch up to their grade level. In this case modifications are made for the purpose of remediating skill gaps.

Intervention

An intervention is a specific program or set of steps to help a student improve in an area of weakness. Instructional interventions focus on subjects like reading and math, and they are designed so the student's progress can be tracked.[8]

One model used in many schools to assess the effectiveness of how a student is being taught is called response to intervention (RTI). The student is first tested to find their current functioning level. After they have received an intervention, their progress is tested again. If the student hasn't improved, the teacher and other educators (the RTI team) select more intensive interventions. This can include meeting with that student's parent(s) to start a process to rule out a learning disability.[9]

Remediation

Remediation is another related term that is often used when targeting foundational skills a student needs to master for a student who has gaps but is in middle school, high school, or at a college level.[10]

See appendix A for more thorough overviews of several common approaches to dyslexia intervention.

Appendix I

Resource Recommendations

Most of the books recommended in this appendix can be purchased at our Wings to Soar website at www.wingstosoaronline.com.

Fresh Perspectives on Dyslexia

In the Mind's Eye: Creative Visual Thinkers, Gifted Dyslexics, and the Rise of Visual Technologies by Thomas G. West

This book highlights the importance of visual thinking as well as visual technologies to help bring out the strong creative potential of individuals with strong visual-spatial skills who may have challenges associated with dyslexia or other learning difficulties. This is the book I highly recommended in chapter 3 for its profiles of 11 famous dyslexics.

The Dyslexic Advantage: Unlocking the Hidden Potential of the Dyslexic Brain by Brock and Fernette Eide, MDs

This is the book that helped me start developing my understanding that the challenges most often associated with dyslexia are directly connected to flip-side strengths. In addition to spending a chapter on each of the M.I.N.D. strengths (Material reasoning, Interconnected reasoning, Narrative reasoning, and Dynamic reasoning), this pair of neuroscientists provides practical suggestions for helping dyslexics with reading and writing. They also overview special focuses and challenges for three stages in a dyslexic's life: the elementary school and middle school years, high school and college, and the workplace.

The Dyslexia Empowerment Plan: A Blueprint for Renewing Your Child's Confidence and Love of Learning by Ben Foss

Ben Foss's own journey as a dyslexic provides helpful insights into the strengths and challenges of being a dyslexic. This book focuses on how to help dyslexics use their individual strengths to learn, not on how to help them learn to eye-read. It also offers help for the parent to coach your child to develop resilience, confidence, self-awareness, and self-advocacy. It helps you understand your rights. It highlights the importance of finding allies for dyslexics so they can feel connected with others with brains wired in a similar manner and know they are not alone.

The Gift of Dyslexia: Why Some of the Smartest People Can't Read... and How They Can Learn by Ronald Davis

If the Davis Dyslexia Correction method overviewed in appendix A sounds like it might be a good fit, this is the book to help you understand more about this unique approach to dyslexia intervention. Whether or not you decide to pursue using this method, the first half of this book will provide new insights into your dyslexic child's unique brain wiring. My main caution is that the description of the Davis Dyslexia Correction method in the second part of the book is detailed enough that you might try it at home with your child; but if it doesn't work, please don't write off the approach, but understand that there are many nuances to doing it effectively, which is why licensed Davis facilitators complete more than 400 hours of training.

"Famous People with Dyslexia" (http://thepowerofdyslexia.com/famous-dyslexics)

It can be empowering to learn about famous people with dyslexia. Here's a good list to start with from The Power of Dys-lex-i-a website.

"An Index of Successful Dyslexics" (http://dyslexia.yale.edu/successfuldyslexics. html?gclid=CjwKEAiA3aW2BRCD_cOo5oCFuUMSJADilMILtztIeytqixGBHrc-mAn4e-VtkJwLfj5JqLi2T1hG3RoC68Hw_wcB)

The Yale Center for Dyslexia and Creativity provides another website with famous dyslexics sorted by categories and links to separate pages with short biographies of each.

More Traditional Perspectives on Dyslexia

International Dyslexia Association (http://www.dyslexiaida.org)

This helpful website provides many useful resources for individuals with dyslexia and parents and teachers helping dyslexics.

International Dyslexia Association's (IDA) Fact Sheets – Dyslexia Basics (http://www. dyslexiaida.org/fact-sheets)

The International Dyslexia Association calls its Fact Sheets "convenient, professionally reviewed materials designed to improve understanding and support advocacy initiatives." The fact sheets are easily accessible on the IDA's website, and they provide easy-to-read synopses of:

- How diagnosis is reached
- Characteristics
- Genetic and neurological information
- General outlook for dyslexics
- References to learn more

The Fact Sheets are expertly written, only slightly jargony and are another must in a parent's or caregiver's "frequently used" file. Having a copy of these fact sheets and any relevant pages from the *DSM-5* regarding your child's diagnosis handy is essential to being confident and accurate when advocating for your child. You might be the only one around the table who can produce some key piece of information.

Basic Facts about Dyslexia and Other Reading Problems by Louisa Cook Moats and Karen Dakin

This is a short book (134 pages) put out by the International Dyslexia Association that provides an overview of dyslexia.

Overcoming Dyslexia: A New and Complete Science-Based Program for Reading Problems at Any Level by Sally Shaywitz, MD

This substantial book (411 pages) offers research-based information about how the brain works, reading problems, and practical techniques that can help dyslexics at any stage overcome their reading challenges. One note is that while some practical strategies are provided that a parent can use at home, Dr. Shaywitz's perspective strongly favors using professional Orton-Gillingham tutors, and this book helps you evaluate whether a reading program or tutor is using solid research-based approaches.

The Dyslexia Checklist: A Practical Reference for Parents and Teachers by Sandra Rief, MA and Judith Stern, MA

This a practical book with lots of tools, strategies, supports, and interventions for parents and teachers to use with dyslexic kids.

Essentials of Dyslexia Assessment and Intervention by Nancy Mather and Barbara Wendling

This book is targeted to professionals who diagnose or help individuals with dyslexia, and as such contains more jargon and formal language. For the parent who likes to do thorough research to thoroughly understand options, and doesn't mind jargon and technical language, it can be useful, as there are many helpful "rapid reference" boxes as well as an extensive 60-page appendix providing descriptions of 26 reading intervention programs they define as evidence-based.

General Learning Concerns

The Mislabeled Child by Brock and Fernette Eide, MDs

If you have concerns about any of the challenges referenced in appendix G that often coexist with dyslexia, this book is my first recommendation for you.

Different Learners by Jane Healy, PhD

If you suspect your child has learning challenges, this book provides understandable explanations of many different learning disorders. It includes some of the latest scientific research on learning, brain function, and genetics as they relate to learning disorders. It can help you identify problems and take appropriate remedial actions both at home and in the school setting.

Meeting the Challenge: Using Love and Logic to Help Children Develop Attention and Behavior Skills by Jim Fay; Foster W. Cline, MD; and Bob Sornson

This book applies "Love and Logic" principles to helping a child with learning, attention, and behavior challenges.

Thinking Differently: An Inspiring Guide for Parents of Children with Learning Disabilities by David Flink

This readable book is written by someone who has dyslexia. It can help you understand your child's diagnosis and help you better advocate for their needs, especially if they will be in a public school setting.

Understood (http://www.understood.org)

This very useful website provides helpful articles and videos about a variety of learning and attention concerns.

LD Online (http://www.ldonline.org)

The LD Online website gathers together for parents and teachers a wealth of information on learning disabilities, learning disorders, and learning differences.

National Center for Learning Disabilities (http://www.ncld.org)

This site provides a collection of helpful resources for parents and teachers of students with learning disabilities, young adults with disabilities, and pediatricians.

Learn the Law, National Center for Learning Disabilities
(http://www.ncld.org/action-center/learn-the-law)

This website summarizes key laws that affect rights and services available to individuals with disabilities.

Wrightslaw (http://www.wrightslaw.com/)

This website should be your go-to resource for everything to do with special education laws and advocacy for your child with special needs.

"The State of Learning Disabilities: Facts, Trends, and Emerging Issues"
(http://www.ncld.org/wp-content/uploads/2014/11/2014-State-of-LD.pdf)

This 2014 52-page report from the National Center for Learning Disabilities was referenced a number of times throughout this book and is a helpful reference.

"A Timeline of Learning and Attention Issues" by Amanda Morin (https://www.understood. org/en/learning-attention-issues/getting-started/what-you-need-to-know/a-timeline-of-learning- and-attention-issues)

This timeline provides an overview of the history of research, special-education laws, and growing public awareness of learning challenges, attention, and dyslexia.

Other Learning Challenges

The Gift of Learning: Proven Methods for Correcting ADD, Math, and Handwriting Problems by Ronald Davis

If your child's struggles have more to do with attention, math, or handwriting rather than reading, spelling, and composition, this book will help you understand the Davis approach to helping with these areas.

Visual Processing and Visual Skills

College of Optometrists in Vision Development (http://www.COVD.org)

The College of Optometrists in Vision Development is the best source for finding a qualified developmental optometrist who can properly evaluate your child's visual processing and visual-skills development and provide vision therapy to treat vision challenges. The website also provides useful checklists and developmental timelines for helping parents identify whether their child needs this more thorough vision evaluation.

See It. Say It. Do It. by Lynn Hellerstein, OD

This book outlines more fully the Developmental Model of Vision summarized in appendix G and is an excellent resource for developing visualization and visual processing skills.

Eyegames: Easy and Fun Visual Exercises by Lois Hickman and Rebecca Hutchins

This book was created by an optometrist and an occupational therapist to provide activities you can do at home to improve vision. However, these activities alone are not sufficient if the child needs visual therapy.

Visual-Spatial Learners: Differentiation Strategies for Creating a Successful Classroom by Alexandra Shires Golon

This book provides lots of practical ideas for helping visual-spatial learners with reading, spelling, handwriting, math facts, organization, and more. While it is targeted to the classroom, most of the ideas can be implemented by parents at home with their children.

Processing Speed

Bright Kids Who Can't Keep Up by Ellen Braaten, PhD; and Brian Willoughby, PhD

This book provides practical help for the parent of a child with slow processing speed.

Executive Functioning

Smart but Scattered and ***Smart but Scattered Teens*** by Peg Dawson, EdD; and Richard Guare, PhD

The first book is a practical guide for parents helping an elementary school or middle school student. The second book is targeted to parents of teens, as the strategies for implementing the same core principles need to change to reflect changing adolescent needs for greater independence.

Late, Lost, and Unprepared: A Parents' Guide to Helping Children with Executive Functioning by Joyce Cooper-Kahn, PhD; and Laurie Dietzel, PhD

This book written by a pair of clinical psychologists is a helpful tool for parents helping disorganized kids on a daily basis.

Highly Sensitive

The Highly Sensitive Child by Elaine Aron, PhD

If you suspect your child may be part of the 20 percent of the population with highly sensitive wiring, I highly recommend this book. Parenting strategies for highly sensitive children are a bit different than those for other children. This book will both help you better understand your highly sensitive child and better support them in an often overwhelming world.

The Highly Sensitive Person by Elaine Aron, PhD

If you are a highly sensitive person yourself, this book by the researcher who identified this trait, which is found in 20 percent of the population (across at least 100 different species), will help you understand that you are not alone in how you experience the world. This book was hugely helpful to me personally in understanding and accepting myself as a highly sensitive person.

The Highly Sensitive Person's Survival Guide by Ted Zeff

This book builds on Elaine Aron's work and provides many practical tips and suggestions for those who are highly sensitive.

Developmental Milestones

As a parent, it can be difficult to know if a concern you are having is actually something to be worried about or just a skill that normally develops at a later stage. The following websites and books gather together lists of timelines of typical development and what to expect at each stage.

The American Speech-Language-Hearing Association (ASHA) (http://www.asha.org/slp/schools/prof-consult/norms)

ASHA has gathered together a collection of websites that provide guidance as to developmental norms for speech and language development.

Michigan Medicine (http://www.med.umich.edu/yourchild/topics/devmile.htm)

Michigan Medicine, from the University of Michigan, has put together a very useful page with developmental milestones from infancy through adolescence.

Your Child's Growing Mind: Brain Development and Learning from Birth through Adolescence by Jane Healy

I recommend that every parent own a copy of this book to reference and understand what is developmentally appropriate for their child to be learning at their current stage of brain development. This is especially important if one or more of your children struggle or are precocious in some area, so you'll know what is typical and what is not.

Slow and Steady Get Me Ready (the "Birth to Age 5" edition) by June R. Oberlander

This book provides brief week-by-week activities to do with your child that help foster skills appropriate for their developmental stage from birth to age five.

Yardsticks: Children in the Classroom Ages 4–14 by Chip Wood

This book is organized by age from ages four to fourteen. Each chapter provides an overview snapshot of a typical child at that age. For each age there are three charts covering typical growth patterns (physical, social-emotional, language, and cognitive), what you can expect to see in the classroom/learning context (vision and fine-motor ability, gross-motor ability, cognitive growth, and social-emotional behavior), and suggestions for age-appropriate curriculum focus (reading, writing, math, and favorite themes).

Teen Stages: ***The Breakthrough Year-by-Year Approach to Understanding Your Ever-Changing Teen*** by Elizabeth and Ken Mellor

This book overviews six distinct stages teens go through (roughly correlated to age) and what teens need from their parents at each of these stages to help them most successfully progress through the stages they typically move through from ages 13 to 21.

Ready or Not, Here Life Comes by Mel Levine, MD

This book is a guide to helping your 12- to 21-year-old get ready to become a successful start-up adult.

Other Helpful Books for Parents

The Whole-Brain Child: 12 Revolutionary Strategies to Nurture Your Child's Developing Mind by Daniel Siegel, MD and Tina Payne Bryson, PhD

I highly recommend all parents read this book, as it makes science about healthy brain development accessible in ways that have practical applications for helping integrate your child's brain development and foster its growth. This book helps you cultivate healthy emotional and intellectual development in your child. It helps you transform everyday interactions with your child in real-life situations into opportunities to actively shape the growth of their brain for the better!

Discover Your Child's Learning Style by Mariaemma Willis and Victoria Kindle Hodson.

This book includes an assessment of multiple aspects of your child's learning style including dispositions, talents, interests, modality, and environment. All of these should play a role in setting up the learning environment at home. Understanding these varied aspects of your child as a learner will help them become the best learner they can be. I especially recommend this book if you are homeschooling.

How Your Child Learns Best: Brain-Friendly Strategies You Can Use to Ignite Your Child's Learning and Increase School Success by Judy Willis, MD, MEd

The unique perspective provided in this book by a neurologist who is also a classroom teacher combines brain research with best classroom practices to improve your child's school success. The practical activities you can do at home with your child to help in all core academic areas are targeted to children ages three to twelve.

How to Talk So Kids Can Learn; How to Talk So Kids Will Listen & Listen So Kids Will Talk; and ***How to Talk So Teens Will Listen & Listen So Teens Will Talk*** by Adele Faber and Elaine Mazlish

These three books all offer very practical advice on effective ways to communicate with your kids.

The Motivation Breakthrough: 6 Secrets to Turning On the Tuned-Out Child by Richard Lavoie

I often hear parents say that their child lacks motivation. This book addresses different motivational styles and provides tips to help you use your child's best motivational style.

It's So Much Work to Be Your Friend by Richard Lavoie

This is an excellent book addressing social skills issues.

Endnotes

Chapter 1: Defining Dyslexia

1. Jessica Becker et al. "Genetic Analysis of Dyslexia Candidate Genes in the European Cross-linguistic NeuroDys Cohort." *European Journal of Human Genetics* 22 (2014): 675-80. *Doi:10.1038/ejhg.2013.199.* http://www.nature.com/ejhg/journal/v22/n5/full/ejhg2013199a.html

2. Natalie R. Powers et al. "Alleles of a Polymorphic ETV6 Binding Site in DCDC2 Confer Risk of Reading and Language Impairment." *The American Journal of Human Genetics* 93.1 (2013): 19-28.

3. Candace Cortiella and Sheldon H. Horowitz, Ed.D. *The State of Learning Disabilities: Facts, Trends and Emerging Issues.* National Center for Learning Disabilities. Third Edition, 2014.

4. Brock L. Eide, M.D., M.A., and Fernette F. Eide, M.D. *The Dyslexic Advantage.* New York: Plume, 2012.

5. International Dyslexia Association. "Dyslexia Basics." 2012. http://www.dyslexiaida.org/dyslexia-basics

6. Ibid.

7. Brock L. Eide, M.D., M.A., and Fernette F. Eide, M.D. *The Dyslexic Advantage.* New York: Plume, 2012.

8. Ibid.

9. Julie Logan. "Dyslexic Entrepreneurs: The Incidence; Their Coping Strategies and Their Business Skills." *Dyslexia* 15.4 (2009): 328-346.

10. Brock L. Eide, M.D., M.A., and Fernette F. Eide, M.D. *The Dyslexic Advantage.* New York: Plume, 2012.

11. Thomas G. West. *Thinking Like Einstein.* Amherst, NY: Prometheus, 2004.

Chapter 2: Redefining Dyslexia: A Fresh Look at the Challenges and the Flip-Side Strengths

1. Thomas G. West. *In the Mind's Eye*. Amherst, NY: Prometheus, 2009.

2. Sally E. Shaywitz et al. "Functional Disruption in the Organization of the Brain for Reading in Dyslexia." *Proceedings of the National Academy of Sciences* 95.5 (1998): 2636-2641.

3. Guinevere F. Eden. *Dyslexia and the Brain*. Baltimore: The International Dyslexia Association (IDA), 2015.

4. Brock L. Eide, M.D., M.A., and Fernette F. Eide, M.D. *The Dyslexic Advantage*. New York: Plume, 2012.

5. Dyslexia Victoria. "Problems of Dyslexia: Right and Left Brain Learning Differences." http://www.dyslexiavictoriaonline.com/parent-s-pages-problems-of-dyslexia

6. Brock L. Eide, M.D., M.A., and Fernette F. Eide, M.D. *The Dyslexic Advantage*. New York: Plume, 2012.

7. Shane Muk. "What Sort of Thinker Are You? Visual or Verbal?" Answers in Genes Blogspot. 2011. http://answersingenes.blogspot.com/2011/04/what-sort-of-thinker-are-you-visual-or.html

8. Discovering Dyslexia. "Dyslexic Thinking Style." http://www.discoveringdyslexia.com/thinkingstyle.html

9. Shane Muk. "What Sort of Thinker Are You? Visual or Verbal?" Answers in Genes Blogspot. 2011. http://answersingenes.blogspot.com/2011/04/what-sort-of-thinker-are-you-visual-or.html

10. Brock L. Eide, M.D., M.A., and Fernette F. Eide, M.D. *The Dyslexic Advantage*. New York: Plume, 2012.

11. Ronald D. Davis. *The Gift of Dyslexia*. New York: Perigree, 2010.

12. Ibid.

13. Emily L. Williams and Manuel F. Casanova. "Autism and Dyslexia: A Spectrum of Cognitive Styles as Defined by Minicolumnar Morphometry." *Medical Hypotheses* 74.1 (2010): 59-62.

14. Ibid.

15. Brock L. Eide, M.D., M.A., and Fernette F. Eide, M.D. *The Dyslexic Advantage*. New York: Plume, 2012.

16. Emily L. Williams and Manuel F. Casanova. "Autism and Dyslexia: A Spectrum of Cognitive Styles as Defined by Minicolumnar Morphometry." *Medical Hypotheses* 74.1 (2010): 59-62.

17. Brock L. Eide, M.D., M.A., and Fernette F. Eide, M.D. *The Dyslexic Advantage*. New York: Plume, 2012.

18. Emily L. Williams and Manuel F. Casanova. "Autism and Dyslexia: A Spectrum of Cognitive Styles as Defined by Minicolumnar Morphometry." *Medical Hypotheses* 74.1 (2010): 59-62.

19. Brock L. Eide, M.D., M.A., and Fernette F. Eide, M.D. *The Dyslexic Advantage*. New York: Plume, 2012.

20. Ibid.

21. Ibid.

22. Ibid.

23. Ronald D. Davis. *The Gift of Dyslexia*. New York: Perigree, 2010.

Chapter 3: Redefining Dyslexia: A Whole-Person View

1. Ben Foss. *The Dyslexia Empowerment Plan: A Blueprint for Renewing Your Child's Confidence and Love of Learning*. New York: Ballantine, 2013.

2. Thomas G. West. *In the Mind's Eye*. Amherst, NY: Prometheus, 2009.

3. International Dyslexia Association. "Dyslexia Basics." 2012. http://www.dyslexiaida.org/dyslexia-basics

4. Thomas G. West. *In the Mind's Eye*. Amherst, NY: Prometheus, 2009.

5. Jack Canfield et al. *The Power of Focus*. Deerfield Beach, FL: HCI Books, 2000.

Chapter 4: Rethinking Learning – Reading

1. National Institutes of Health. "National Reading Panel." https://www.nichd.nih.gov/research/supported/Pages/nrp.aspx

2. Wiley Blevins. "Understanding Phonics." Scholastic Teaching Resources. https://www.scholastic.com/teachers/article/understanding-phonics

3. K12 Reader. "Phonemic Awareness vs. Phonological Awareness." http://www.k12reader.com/phonemic-awareness-vs-phonological-awareness

4. Ibid.

5. Brock L. Eide, M.D., M.A., and Fernette F. Eide, M.D. *The Dyslexic Advantage*. New York: Plume, 2012.

6. Ronald D. Davis. *The Gift of Dyslexia*. New York: Perigree, 2010.

7. Ibid.

Chapter 5: Rethinking Learning – Spelling

1. Susan C. Anthony. *Spelling Plus: 1000 Words toward Spelling Success*. Anchorage, AK: Instructional Resources, 1999.

Chapter 6: Rethinking Learning – Writing

1. Jennifer Heidl-Knoblock and Jody Dale. "The Six Traits Professional Development Model." Iron Mountain Schools. 2005. http://www.imschools.org/uploads/4/0/8/7/40873415/overview6traits.pdf

2. Education Northwest. "Trait Definitions." http://educationnorthwest.org/traits/trait-definitions

3. Dave Kemper, Patrick Sebranek, and Verne Meyer. *Write Source*. Wilmington, MA: Great Source Education Group, 2005.

4. Douglas Fisher and Nancy Frey. *Better Learning through Structured Teaching*. Alexandria, VA: ASCD, 2013.

5. Alabama State Department. of Education. "Definition of Narrative Writing." http://web.alsde.edu/general/AnnotatedPackets/20082009/Grade10AnnotatedExemplars-2.pdf

Appendix B: Leveling the Playing Field through Accommodations

1. PACER Center. "School Accommodation and Modification Ideas for Students Who Receive Special Education Services." 2015. http://www.pacer.org/parent/php/PHP-c49a.pdf

2. Lisa Nielsen. "Advice for Teaching Keyboard." The Innovative Educator Blogspot. 2011. http://theinnovativeeducator.blogspot.com/2011/02/when-should-students-start-learning-to.html

Appendix C: Teaching Principles, Strategies, and Tools

1. Jack Canfield et al. *The Power of Focus*. Deerfield Beach, FL: HCI Books, 2000.

2. Mel Levine. *A Mind at a Time*. New York: Simon & Schuster, 2002.

3. John Ratey. S*park: The Revolutionary New Science of Exercise and the Brain*. Boston, MA: Little, Brown and Company, 2008

4. Jay McTighe and Grant Wiggins. "Essential Questions." ASCD. http://www.ascd.org/publications/books/109004/chapters/What-Makes-a-Question-Essential%A2.aspx

Appendix D: Expanded Multisensory Practice

1. Susan C. Anthony. *Spelling Plus: 1000 Words toward Spelling Success*. Anchorage, AK: Instructional Resources, 1999.

Appendix G: Challenges that Often Co-Exist with Dyslexia

1. American Speech-Language-Hearing Association. "Language-Based Learning Disabilities." 2016. http://www.asha.org/public/speech/disorders/LBLD.htm

2. Patricia W. Newhall. *Language-Based Teaching Series: Language-Based Learning Disabilities*. Prides Crossing, MA: Landmark School Outreach Program, 2012.

3. Louise Spear-Swerling. "Specific Language Impairment." LD Online. WETA. 2006. http://www.ldonline.org/spearswerling/Specific_Language_Impairment

4. Virginia W. Beringer, Ph.D. and Beverly Wolf, M.Ed. *Understanding Dysgraphia*. Baltimore, MD: International Dyslexia Association (IDA), 2012.

5. Teri James Bellis, Ph.D. "Understanding Auditory Processing Disorders in Children." American Speech-Language-Hearing Association. 2016. http://www.asha.org/public/hearing/ Understanding-Auditory-Processing-Disorders-in-Children

6. Ibid.

7. The Understood Team. "Understanding Auditory Processing Disorder." 2016. http://www. understood.org/en/learning-attention-issues/child-learning-disabilities/auditory-processing-disorder/understanding-auditory-processing-disorder

8. Candace Cortiella and Sheldon H. Horowitz, Ed.D. "The State of Learning Disabilities: Facts, Trends and Emerging Issues." National Center for Learning Disabilities. Third Edition, 2014.

9. Teri James Bellis, Ph.D. "Understanding Auditory Processing Disorders in Children." American Speech-Language-Hearing Association. ASHA. 2016. http://www.asha.org/public/hearing/ Understanding-Auditory-Processing-Disorders-in-Children

10. Ibid.

11. The Understood Team. "Understanding Auditory Processing Disorder." 2016. http://www. understood.org/en/learning-attention-issues/child-learning-disabilities/auditory-processing-disorder/understanding-auditory-processing-disorder

12. Teri James Bellis, Ph.D. "Understanding Auditory Processing Disorders in Children." American Speech-Language-Hearing Association. 2016. http://www.asha.org/public/hearing/ Understanding-Auditory-Processing-Disorders-in-Children

13. Lynn F. Hellerstein, O.D. *See It. Say It. Do It.* Centennial, CO: High Clear Publishing, 2010.

14. Ibid.

15. The Understood Team. "Vision Therapy and Dyslexia: What You Need to Know." https://www. understood.org/en/learning-attention-issues/treatments-approaches/alternative-therapies/ vision-therapy-what-it-is-and-how-it-works

16. Lois Hickman and Rebecca Hutchins. *Eyegames: Easy and Fun Visual Exercises.* Arlington, TX: Sensory World, 2010.

17. Ellen Braaten, Ph.D. and Brian Willoughby, Ph.D. *Bright Kids Who Can't Keep Up*. New York: The Guilford Press, 2014.

18. Joyce Cooper-Kahn and Laurie Dietzel. *Late, Lost, and Unprepared*. Bethesda, MD: Woodbine House, 2008.

19. Amanda Morin. "Understanding Executive Functioning Issues." Understood. 2014. https://www.understood.org/en/learning-attention-issues/child-learning-disabilities/executive-functioning-issues/understanding-executive-functioning-issues

20. Ibid.

21. Candace Cortiella and Sheldon H. Horowitz, Ed.D. "The State of Learning Disabilities: Facts, Trends and Emerging Issues." National Center for Learning Disabilities. Third Edition, 2014.

22. Ibid.

23. International Dyslexia Association. "Attention-Deficit/Hyperactivity Disorder (AD/HD) and Dyslexia Fact Sheet." 2008. https://dyslexiaida.org/attention-deficithyperactivity-disorder-adhd-and-dyslexia

24. Candace Cortiella and Sheldon H. Horowitz, Ed.D. "The State of Learning Disabilities: Facts, Trends and Emerging Issues." National Center for Learning Disabilities. Third Edition, 2014.

25. Mayo Clinic. "Attention-Deficit/Hyperactivity Disorder (ADHD) in Children." 2016. http://www.mayoclinic.org/diseases-conditions/adhd/basics/symptoms/con-20023647

26. Rosemary Tannock. "Inattention and Working Memory: Effects on Academic Performance." 2008. *Handbook of Executive Functioning*. New York: Springer, 2014. p. 472.

27. Pearson Education. "Working Memory Checklist." http://www.cogmed.com/working-memory-checklist

28. Brock L. Eide, M.D., M.A., and Fernette F. Eide, M.D. *The Dyslexic Advantage*. New York: Plume, 2012.

29. Candace Cortiella and Sheldon H. Horowitz, Ed.D. "The State of Learning Disabilities: Facts, Trends and Emerging Issues." National Center for Learning Disabilities. Third Edition, 2014.

Appendix H: Making Sense of Jargon

1. U.S. Dept. of Education. "Thirty-Five Years of Progress in Educating Children with Disabilities through IDEA." 2010. https://www2.ed.gov/about/offices/list/osers/idea35/history/idea-35-history.pdf

2. Candace Cortiella and Sheldon H. Horowitz, Ed.D. "The State of Learning Disabilities: Facts, Trends and Emerging Issues." National Center for Learning Disabilities. Third Edition, 2014.

3. American Psychiatric Association. *Diagnostic and Statistical Manual of Mental Disorders, 5th Edition*. Arlington, VA: American Psychiatric Publishing, 2013.

4. Laura Robb. "What Is Differentiated Instruction?" excerpted from *Differentiating Reading Instruction*. Wilkinsburg, PA: Scholastic Teaching Resources, 2008. http://www.scholastic.com/teachers/article/what-differentiated-instruction

5. PACER Center. "School Accommodation and Modification Ideas for Students Who Receive Special Education Services." 2015. http://www.pacer.org/parent/php/PHP-c49a.pdf

6. Ibid.

7. Ibid.

8. Andrew M. I. Lee. "Instructional Intervention: What You Need to Know." Understood. https://www.understood.org/en/learning-attention-issues/treatments-approaches/educational-strategies/instructional-intervention-what-you-need-to-know

9. Special Education Guide. "Response to Intervention." 2016. http://www.specialeducationguide.com/pre-k-12/response-to-intervention

10. Andrew M. I. Lee. "Instructional Intervention: What You Need to Know." Understood. https://www.understood.org/en/learning-attention-issues/treatments-approaches/educational-strategies/instructional-intervention-what-you-need-to-know

Acknowledgments

've been blessed with the support of many wonderful people over the years with whom I've developed my expertise in working with outside-the-box learners. So many have provided practical support and shown patience and long-suffering in the months it took to write this book.

Thank you to Christine Kloser and your professional yet compassionate team. I could not have done this without the structure of your Get Your Book Done program and the support of the MasterHeart program. I am amazed by my own personal transformation through this team's focus and help in the process of writing my book.

Thank you, Carrie Jareed, for your guidance through the publishing process. Thanks to my editorial team, Michelle Cohen and Gwen Hoffnagle, for making sure we got all of it correct.

Thank you to Jean Marie, Marilynn Nash, and several of my clients for feedback on early drafts. Thank you, Sarah Binger, for doing detailed editing and rework suggestions to help me get the book ready to submit to my publisher. And a huge thank you to Shannon Greaves for extensive editing and revision support and writing the core of the writing chapter. Thank you, Ben Nash and Marilynn Nash, for your help proofreading the book.

Thank you to my professional colleagues, Teri Krueger, Shannon Greaves, Erin Smilkstein, and Georgia Smith, who have worked with me at Hope Academy and Wings to Soar Online Academy to continue to develop our unique approach to education for outside-the-box learners. I know it hasn't always been easy, and I couldn't have done it without you.

Thank you to the hundreds of students I've worked with; I've learned so much from you. Thank you, parents, for trusting me with your children.

I want to extend a special thanks to my dad, Brian Yocom, who has believed in me all these years and served as a sounding board so many times as I've worked with students and tried out new programs and approaches, and through the process of writing, revising, and editing this book.

My kitty therapists, Sam and Frodo, have been my faithful companions through the many long hours spent on the computer.

And a great big thank you goes to my dear husband, Daniel Nash, for loving and supporting me through nearly 20 years of marriage. Your support has allowed me time, emotional support, and financial resources to devote to research and growing the school. I couldn't have done it without you.

About the Author

Beth Ellen Nash has her education degree from the University of Wisconsin–Madison and has 17 years' experience working with struggling learners. She was the founder, director, and lead teacher for eight years at Hope Academy, a school for struggling middle school and high school students in Madison, Wisconsin.

In 2011 she shifted toward an individualized online and homeschool hybrid option and founded Wings to Soar Online Academy, specializing in the creation of Path to Success™ Personalized Learning Plans for dyslexics and other outside-the-box learners from kindergarten through 12th grade.

Beth Ellen is currently Curriculum Coordinator, Intervention Specialist, and Integrated Liberal Studies teacher for Wings to Soar Online Academy. She has tutored, assessed, and consulted with hundreds of families and companies that serve homeschoolers as well as public charter schools. She is the author of *Wings to Soar: Integrated, Multisensory Language Arts with Words You Really Use*. She is a sought-after speaker for many homeschooling and educational conferences. She tailors her talks to the needs of the audience, drawing on her experience with students ages 3 to 21 with dyslexia, ADHD, autism spectrum, RAD, OCD, anxiety, depression, and learning disabilities, and those who otherwise learn differently from traditional schooling.

Made in the USA
Coppell, TX
15 February 2022

73613925R00131